Short-Term Memory Loss:

Using The Power Of Sales To Improve Life, Advance Your Career & Build Life Changing Wealth

By Ian S. Hoover

Dedication:

In heartfelt gratitude, this book, my initial venture into the world of writing, is dedicated to my mother, Lois. Without her unwavering influence, I would not have grown into the man I am today. She exemplified true strength, battling Muscular Dystrophy without ever offering excuses. Her actions taught me invaluable lessons on how to treat others and how to make the most of any circumstance. Despite facing financial limitations, she poured her heart into raising me and became an extraordinary mother, and Nama (Grandmother) to my incredible children. Though I may not always devote enough time to her these days, she never makes me feel guilty for focusing on my business, family, and life. Her support and teachings have been instrumental in shaping who I am today. Thank you, Mom, for your unwavering presence, your guidance, your steadfast support, and for being the greatest mother in the world. Your sacrifices will forever be acknowledged and cherished by me.

About the Author:

Ian Hoover, a dynamic entrepreneur, defies the odds and epitomizes the power of resilience and determination. Born and raised in the gritty surroundings of Erie, Pennsylvania, his childhood was shaped by the challenges and adversity that often accompany such environments. Growing up in a rough mobile home park, where drugs, aggressive dogs, and dilapidated homes were the norm, Ian experienced firsthand the harsh realities of his surroundings.

Raised by a single mother who battles Muscular Dystrophy, Ian learned the true meaning of strength and perseverance from an early age. Despite her disability, his mother overcame every obstacle and instilled in him the values of hard work, resourcefulness, and the unwavering belief that one's circumstances need not define their future. He fondly recalls her ability to stretch a meager budget, humorously remarking that she could conjure up a hundred ways to prepare potatoes, thanks to their affordability and bulk purchases.

It was his mother who imparted a critical life lesson upon Ian—a lesson that would shape his trajectory and become the catalyst for his incredible success. She taught him that there were two fields that would always offer opportunities for employment: medicine and sales. While medicine didn't ignite his passion, the allure of sales and the art of connecting with people sparked a fire within him.

From that moment on, Ian embarked on a relentless pursuit of knowledge and mastery in the realm of sales. He honed his skills, discovered effective strategies, and cultivated an unshakeable belief in his ability to influence and create meaningful connections. Armed with these invaluable attributes, he ventured forth into the world, seeking opportunities and creating his own path to success.

Today, as a thriving entrepreneur, owner of multiple businesses, and a testament to the transformative power of sales, Ian is driven by a passion to share his knowledge and experiences with others. Through his first ever book, "Short-Term Memory Loss: Using The Power Of Sales To Improve Life, Advance Your Career & Build Life Changing Wealth" he seeks to empower individuals from all walks of life. He imparts the lessons he has learned and demonstrates that sales is a gateway to not only financial prosperity but also personal growth and fulfillment.

Ian Hoover's story serves as a powerful reminder that success knows no bounds and that with the right mindset, unwavering determination, and the willingness to embrace the art of sales, anyone can rise above their circumstances to create an extraordinary life.

Introduction

Sales permeates our everyday lives, constantly making its presence known. I find myself contemplating its influence wherever I go. For instance, during a recent visit to Starbucks, I observed the following:

1. As I approached the entrance, my attention was drawn to one or two window clings showcasing new products.
2. En route to the counter, an array of mugs and gifts caught my eye, some of which were conveniently labeled as "on sale."
3. A well-placed cooler, conveniently located before reaching the counter, offered a tempting selection of refreshing snacks and beverages.
4. The person ahead of me in line sported a shirt displaying his company's logo, subtly promoting their brand.
5. Adjacent to the counter, an enticing display case showcased an assortment of delectable muffins and pastries.
6. Prominently positioned on the counter was a gift card available for purchase.
7. Strategically placed signs adorned the area behind the counter, proudly highlighting their latest drink

offerings. Repetition increases the likelihood of us trying something we have encountered multiple times.

8. Upon payment, the credit card machine encouraged me to download their app for exclusive perks.
9. The staff member behind the counter sported a pin showcasing a new drink, serving as a gentle reminder of its presence.
10. An enticing offer presented itself: for a mere 80 cents more, I could upgrade to a venti-sized beverage.
11. Before bidding me farewell, I was kindly handed a coupon for a half-priced drink if I returned after 2 pm.
12. As I made my way to collect my drink, bags of coffee beans tempted me from the counter, enticing me with the option to purchase them whole or freshly ground. Additionally, a special promotion was in effect, further piquing my interest.

These subtle yet pervasive sales tactics surround us, shaping our choices and experiences in ways we may not always consciously realize. Rest assured, Starbucks is not the sole practitioner of such techniques; all companies employ similar strategies consistently. Why? Simply because they work, even if not with absolute certainty, they boast a notable success rate.

Take Panera, for example. They have recently introduced a coffee club membership at an affordable monthly price, around ten dollars. By availing yourself of this offer and visiting Panera daily, you can save a substantial sum on coffee and other beverages. However, it is crucial to recognize that this initiative primarily aims to drive customer footfall, enticing them to visit more frequently than they previously might have. Once inside, Panera endeavors to entice you with additional offerings, effectively maximizing their sales opportunities. Even their self-service tablet prompts customers with three upsells before granting them their complimentary coffee.

In a world where success seems reserved for the chosen few, where opportunities appear to favor the privileged, and where dreams can wither away in the face of adversity, there exists a powerful equalizer—an art form that knows no boundaries and a skill set that transcends backgrounds and limitations. That art form is sales, and it holds the key to unlocking unimaginable potential within each of us.

Welcome to "Short-Term Memory Loss: Using The Power Of Sales To Improve Life, Advance Your Career & Build Life Changing Wealth" a book that shatters the myth that you need a fancy degree, impeccable credentials, or extraordinary luck to achieve financial prosperity and personal fulfillment. This is a guidebook designed to prove that anyone, armed with the ability to engage in meaningful conversations, can harness the transformative power of sales to revolutionize their lives.

Within the pages of this book, you will embark on a journey—one that traces the remarkable trajectory of an uneducated kid from the depths of the ghetto to becoming a successful entrepreneur, commanding an empire of businesses, and amassing a fortune of nearly ten million dollars by his mid-thirties. That kid is me. I stand before you as living proof that hard work, unwavering determination, and the invaluable skills I am about to impart can alter the course of your existence.

This is not a tale of overnight success, or shortcuts to riches. No, this is a testament to the immense potential that resides within each and every one of us. It's about seizing the power of connection, persuasion, and influence—the core tenets of sales—and channeling them towards creating a life of abundance, freedom, and fulfillment.

In the chapters ahead, you will learn how to navigate the intricate dance of human interaction, uncovering the secrets of effective communication, building rapport, and mastering the art of negotiation. You will discover strategies to overcome rejection, turn setbacks into stepping stones, and transform obstacles into opportunities.

But this book is more than a manual for financial success; it is a call to action. It is a clarion call for you to believe in yourself, to recognize your worth, and to embrace the immense potential that lies dormant within you. It is a reminder that regardless of your past circumstances or present limitations, you possess the innate ability to shape your own destiny and create a life of immeasurable wealth and purpose.

So, are you ready to embark on this extraordinary journey? Are you prepared to leave behind the shackles of doubt, uncertainty, and mediocrity? If so, let the transformation begin. Through the teachings and experiences shared in this book you will uncover the key to unlocking your true potential and embrace a future brimming with limitless possibilities.

Get ready to revolutionize your life, as we embark on a remarkable voyage together—one that will forever alter the way you perceive sales, success, and the extraordinary wealth that awaits you.

Chapter 1: Take Action

"Short term memory loss is a salesman's best tool "- Ian
Hoover

The title "Short Term Memory Loss" for this book holds a
significant meaning rooted in my experience as a salesperson
and valuable insight gained through my time at T-Mobile. It
was in this period I coined the phrase "Short term memory loss
is a salesman's best tool," imparting a crucial lesson to my
team.

During my time in retail management, I frequently
encountered irate customers whose phones were
malfunctioning, and who would go to great lengths to disrupt
my day. Despite the challenges, I possessed a remarkable
ability to resolve their issues and ensure their departure with a
sense of satisfaction. However, it's important to acknowledge
that it is impossible to please everyone. I have been subjected
to name-calling and even threats to my personal safety, all due
to a seemingly trivial matter like a cell phone.

When viewed from their perspective, the cell phone represents
an integral part of their lives, comparable in significance to
their home or vehicle. Consequently, their frustration and
anger are understandable. Nonetheless, it is crucial not to
allow a single disgruntled individual to ruin your day.

Succumbing to such negativity would not only affect your emotional well-being but also result in financial consequences. Allowing frustration to impact your performance can subsequently hinder your sales and, consequently, your earnings for the day.

In sales, rejection and negative interactions are an inevitable part of the process. However, to succeed, it is essential to cultivate a mindset of short-term memory loss. This means not allowing one bad experience, or rejection, to linger and impact your confidence, or future interactions. Instead, it is about learning from each encounter, adapting your approach, and approaching each new opportunity with a fresh perspective.

By adopting this mindset, you empower yourself to move forward, maintain resilience, and stay focused on your ultimate goal: closing deals and achieving success. "Short Term Memory Loss" encapsulates this valuable lesson and serves as a reminder that, as a salesperson, your ability to let go of setbacks quickly and maintain a positive mindset is an invaluable tool for achieving sales success.

In the pursuit of success, there is a fundamental principle that reigns supreme—the power of taking action. It is the catalyst that propels dreams into reality and transforms aspirations into tangible achievements. In this chapter, we delve into the crucial first step on the path to greatness.

From a tender age, I understood the significance of taking action. At just eleven years old, I embarked on a paper route, delivering news to the doorsteps of my community. But it wasn't merely about the task itself; it was about how I approached it. By treating my clients with respect, going the extra mile, and providing exceptional service, I transformed a simple paper route into a lucrative enterprise. Each year, during the holiday season,I earned over $600 in cash and received numerous generous gifts. The local newspaper, recognizing my outstanding dedication, even featured me as one of their top paper carriers.

As I grew older, my thirst for success intensified. At sixteen, I found myself juggling full-time employment at a bustling truck stop, which housed the busiest Subway restaurant in America at the time, with the pressures every teen experiences.. Even with the demands of playing sports and the desire to own a car, I immersed myself in the relentless pursuit of financial independence. Looking back, I sometimes wish I had savored the carefree moments of my youth, but that period of hard work and minimal sleep instilled within me an unparalleled work ethic that would catapult my career.

In my late teens, I found myself working at Best Buy, where I learned the fundamentals of selling, and upselling, to customers. It was there that my innate ability to build relationships, and seize opportunities, led me to become one of the top salespeople in our region, earning nearly six figures at the tender age of eighteen. However, I must admit, I made a crucial mistake during this time—I squandered that hard-earned money on a lavish lifestyle and failed to invest it wisely.

It was a book called "Rich Dad Poor Dad" that served as a wake-up call. It revealed the importance of using the money earned from sales as a means to generate wealth through investments. Heeding this newfound wisdom, I made my first significant investment at nineteen—a home worth a modest $30,000. Little did I know that this humble abode would turn out to be one of my most successful investments, one that I still own to this day.

This book isn't just about teaching you how to sell; it is about encouraging you to take massive action. It is ultimately about finding the sales vehicle that can generate substantial income and then going above and beyond, hustling relentlessly. It doesn't stop there. You must also invest that hard-earned capital into assets that have the potential to build massive wealth for you and your family, even for generations to come.

Taking action isn't just a mantra; it's the essence of my journey. It can be said it started with my relentless pursuit of a job at Best Buy. Not receiving a response to my initial application, I refused to accept defeat. Instead, I applied three times a day until they finally called me. Each application took over half an hour, complete with a personality assessment. When I eventually received the eagerly awaited call, the lady on the other end of the line scheduling my interview asked me to stop applying. In a stroke of unexpected serendipity, the general manager of the store even stepped in during my third interview to meet the determined young man who had applied over twenty times. It was at that moment I realized no obstacle could stand in my way if I simply refused to take no for an answer.

Every journey starts somewhere, and this process will not make you instantly rich. It requires building and grinding day after day. It demands setting goals and posting them in places where you will see them every day, reinforcing your vision.

Before embarking on the path to success, it is essential to have a general idea of the direction you want to take. Consider a few examples to illustrate this point. Starting in retail, for instance, you can begin by researching high-paying commission-based jobs in the industry. Identify the companies that offer the most lucrative opportunities and submit applications to each of them. Do not stop there—go the extra mile by personally delivering your resume to the managers of these locations. Engage them in conversations about when they plan to fill the position, and provide compelling reasons why you would be an exceptional addition to their team.

Remember, when selling yourself, the key is to focus on WIFM (What's In It For Me) from the employer's perspective. Craft a pitch that highlights the value you bring to their team and the benefits they stand to gain by hiring you. Securing the interview is just the beginning.

To stand out from the competition, you must embrace the power of relentless follow-up. Be the squeaky wheel that gets the grease. After the initial application and in-person visit, follow up with an email to thank the hiring manager for their time and the opportunity to discuss their amazing position. A few days later, make another phone call, providing a valid reason for reaching out, such as technical issues with your phone. Apologize for any inconvenience caused and seize the moment to inquire if they can schedule an interview while you have their valuable attention.

This unwavering commitment and relentless behavior will force hiring managers to take a closer look at you. In a world filled with individuals who settle for mediocrity, your persistence and determination will set you apart, demonstrating that you are the candidate they need on their team.

Once you have secured a position, the journey is far from over. To progress and ascend within your chosen career, you must strive to be the best at what you do. Make your aspirations and goals known to your superiors in a polite and respectful manner. Let them understand that your intention is to become a role model, teaching and inspiring others to reach their full potential, just as they have done for you.

But excellence is not attained overnight. It requires continuous effort and dedication. As you build your career, you will inevitably encounter ceilings and limitations within your current role. When that happens, it is time to set your sights on the next, more profitable opportunity.

It is important to express your goals and aspirations to your superiors in a respectful and tactful manner. As you progress in your career, continue to build it up until you have reached its full potential. In my own experience at T-Mobile, the company had certain requirements for promotion, such as being bilingual; maintaining a certain physical appearance, which included orthodontics; and obtaining additional qualifications or a degree. While I recognized the limitations and saw colleagues spending years striving for that elusive next level, I knew it was time for me to explore new opportunities.

This realization marks the beginning of seeking the next step in your career journey. You can repeat the process outlined earlier, but this time consider venturing into higher-end products or industries that offer greater commission potential, such as pharmaceutical sales or real estate. While numerous options exist, it is crucial to demonstrate your sales experience to prospective employers. In my case, having received multiple awards from T-Mobile, including being recognized in the esteemed "Winners Circle" as one of the top 2% in sales nationwide in 2008, undoubtedly set me apart in subsequent interview processes.

Mentorship plays a crucial role in accelerating your journey towards success. If you aspire to enter the world of real estate investing, consider a strategy called wholesaling—a method that does not require a license but can yield substantial profits by flipping contracts to real estate investors. To break into this field, approach the best wholesalers in your area and offer to work for them in exchange for mentorship. Emphasize your willingness to learn and contribute your time and energy to their business. Be persistent in your pursuit, even resorting to tactics like driving for dollars—identifying potential properties for your mentor and presenting them with a detailed list of prospects. Show them that you are committed to putting in the time and effort that their business requires.

One movie that has left a lasting impression on me is "The Wolf of Wall Street." If you haven't seen it yet, I highly recommend it. While many viewers may watch the film and see Jordan Belfort as a scoundrel, there's a valuable lesson to be learned from his relentless pursuit of success. Despite his questionable ethics, what stood out to me was his resolute determination and his ability to transform ordinary individuals in to exceptional salespeople. I firmly believe that if he had embraced a moral compass, he could have achieved tremendous success through legal means.

"The Wolf of Wall Street" showcases numerous sales skills and abilities. However, one of Jordan's greatest strengths, particularly early in his career, was his willingness to take massive action. When faced with being laid off from Wall Street, most people would have never considered taking a job in penny stocks. Yet, not only did Jordan take that opportunity, but he also maximized its potential through the incredible commissions they offered. His ability to seize opportunities and make the most of them was truly remarkable.

"The Wolf of Wall Street" also emphasizes the power of a compelling sales script. A well-crafted script not only helps you secure initial contact with potential customers but also enables you to stay on track and make efficient sales calls. In sales, time is of the essence, and lengthy conversations can hinder your productivity. Instead, it's crucial to get on the phone, deliver your message effectively, secure the appointment or desired outcome, and move on to the next call.

In this book, we will delve deeper into the art of sales scripts, exploring strategies to create persuasive and concise scripts that capture attention, address customer needs, and lead to successful outcomes. Mastering the art of scripting will empower you to make the most of every interaction and maximize your sales potential.

In the pursuit of success, obstacles and failures are inevitable. Many renowned figures, such as Michael Jordan, Emmitt Smith, Bill Gates, Jim Carrey, and Benjamin Franklin, encountered their fair share of setbacks before achieving greatness. Michael Jordan was initially cut from his high school basketball team, Emmitt Smith was told he was too small for the NFL, Bill Gates faced failure with his first business venture, Jim Carrey experienced homelessness, and Benjamin Franklin dropped out of school at a young age.

Similarly, I faced adversity when I was fired from T-Mobile while my wife was pregnant with our second child. These examples serve as powerful reminders that setbacks are not the end of the road but rather opportunities for growth and resilience. When faced with obstacles and failures, it is crucial to rise above them, dust yourself off, and continue taking massive action towards your goals.

During the COVID-19 pandemic, Pennsylvania stood out as the sole state in the USA that classified real estate as "non-essential." Consequently, I found myself unable to operate my business, as doing so would have incurred substantial fines, potentially leading to its closure. I have never been one to idly pass time watching television, so I took the opportunity to embark on a side venture. I began purchasing primarily broken electronics, repairing them, and reselling them for a profit. Over the course of the sixty-day period when my main business was on hold, I invested around three thousand dollars in inventory. Through dedicated effort, I managed to convert that into approximately $7,500, yielding a net profit of $4,500. I devoted roughly twenty to thirty hours per week to this endeavor. While I didn't necessarily require the additional four thousand dollars, it certainly proved beneficial. Engaging in this side hustle allowed me to occupy my mind, diverting it from the prevailing negativity in the world at that moment.

Expanding on this experience, even after resuming my main business activities, I still possessed an inventory worth approximately one thousand dollars or more. Consequently, I decided to offer this inventory to my friend David, who was seeking a side venture. Initially, Dave performed admirably, generating around $1,500 for each of us over the course of a month. Encouraged by our success, I reinvested the proceeds into acquiring more inventory. Unfortunately, Dave eventually gave up, citing various excuses for his inability to continue. I hold a deep fondness for Dave, as he is truly one of my closest friends with our friendship dating back to the third grade. However, I cannot impart upon him my own hunger and drive. Considering the amount of money Dave earns from his day job, there existed a possibility that we could have replaced his income and expanded the business.

Some individuals are simply not suited for entrepreneurship. Reflecting upon the situation, it's worth noting that despite having someone willing to invest capital, an established system, and ample inventory, Dave succumbed to excuses. Consequently, we are likely still sitting on several thousand dollars' worth of inventory, which will remain untouched and unsold. The question then arises: Will you be like Dave, or will you refuse to let excuses hinder your progress? Keep your focus on the ultimate goal of your journey, and instead of saying "I can't," challenge yourself with the question, "How can I?"

In this journey, you will encounter challenges, face rejection, and experience moments of doubt. However, by persevering and maintaining a resilient mindset, you can overcome these hurdles and achieve tremendous success. Remember, success is often born out of the willingness to embrace challenges and the determination to keep moving forward, no matter the circumstances.

Chapter 2: The Art of Sales

"97% of the people who quit too soon are employed by the 3% who never gave up" - Jordan Belfot

Sales is an art form that requires dedication, practice, and the ability to adapt and refine your approach. In my early days of making expired listing calls as a realtor, I was far from perfect. I vividly remember how terrible I was during those initial calls, wishing I had recorded them for posterity. However, I didn't let my shortcomings discourage me. Instead, I recognized the need for improvement and set out to master the art of persuasion.

Formulating a script became my guiding light. I diligently crafted a script, making revisions and adjustments until it resonated with potential clients. To hone my skills, I committed to making over one hundred sales calls each day, Monday through Saturday, from nine in the morning to eleven. It was through consistent practice and persistence that I began to see progress.

The credit I can give to my 23-year-old self is the refusal to give up. I remained determined, continuously refining the script until it became a powerful tool. Eventually, it became ingrained in my memory, allowing me to make calls effortlessly and without the need for a computer. This newfound mastery of the script enabled me to make sales calls even while driving between appointments, maximizing my productivity.

At T-Mobile USA, where I achieved a position among the top 2% of salespeople in the company, I utilized various strategies to excel. While my coworkers would idle around, engaging in gossip or playing on their phones during slow periods, I took a different approach. I positioned myself at the front of the store, eagerly engaging with customers before anyone else could. I also made a point to build relationships with other individuals working in the mall, recognizing the potential for additional sales opportunities.

The art of sales extends beyond a mere transaction. It involves the artistry of building connections, understanding customers' needs, and delivering value. It requires seizing opportunities, even during challenging times. By cultivating a mastery of sales techniques and developing a keen sense of timing, you can elevate your artistry as a salesperson and stand out among the competition.

Indeed, the nuances and small details can make a significant difference in sales. In the wireless store where I worked, I developed a keen sense of observation and the ability to read the line of customers. Understanding the subtle cues and behaviors of customers allowed me to identify potential sales opportunities and prioritize my approach.

During busy periods, I would carefully assess the line of customers, observing their actions and demeanor. For example, if the third person in line was discussing activation or holding a rate plan brochure, it indicated a potential sale in progress. On the other hand, if the second person appeared upset and held a broken phone or a bill, it signified an issue that wouldn't lead to any commission. Recognizing these indicators helped me manage my time effectively and ensure I could seize potential sales while handling current clients.

However, it was inevitable that I would encounter customers with issues or those seeking to make bill payments. In those instances, I utilized my problem-solving abilities to address their concerns efficiently. Simultaneously, I leveraged the opportunity to build a relationship with the customer. By carefully auditing their account, I could identify additional lines they could add or outdated phones that could be upgraded. Every interaction presented a chance to transform it into a potential sale by providing personalized recommendations and demonstrating the value they would gain.

These subtle techniques, such as reading the line and maximizing every customer interaction, were part of my approach to sales. They enabled me to go beyond the transactional aspect and foster meaningful connections with customers. By focusing on understanding their needs and offering tailored solutions, I consistently found opportunities to enhance their experience and generate sales.

While reading the line and prioritizing potential sales may have caused some tension among my coworkers, it was a strategic approach rather than an unethical one. I understood the importance of utilizing my time effectively to maximize my commissions and provide for my family. It's crucial to remember that in the world of sales, our primary focus should be on our own success and financial well-being.

It is true that we are not in the workplace solely to make friends, although I did have the fortune of forming deep and lasting friendships with some of my colleagues who shared the same drive and ambition. These individuals have become an invaluable part of my life and continue to support and inspire me to this day.

While it is important to maintain professional relationships, it is equally important not to let the fear of upsetting your competition hinder your own progress. We must prioritize our own success and take actions that position us for the greatest possible achievements. This doesn't mean engaging in shady or unethical practices, but rather focusing on utilizing effective strategies and making the most of every opportunity.

In the competitive sales arena, it is crucial to remember that our main responsibility is to ourselves and our loved ones. By channeling our energy into maximizing our potential, we can ensure financial stability and provide for our families. We must find that balance between being respectful and supportive of our colleagues while also striving to achieve our personal goals.

Identifying your own strengths and capitalizing on them is essential in the art of sales. Every individual possesses unique qualities that can be harnessed to build relationships, establish trust, and influence customers' decisions. Whether it is your ability to connect with people on a personal level, your knowledge and expertise in a specific area, or your talent for persuasive communication, recognizing and utilizing these skills will set you apart from your competitors.

During my time of making numerous sales calls daily, I frequently encountered expired listings belonging to a particular agent. This agent, Tim, possessed outstanding interpersonal skills and a likable personality. His clients genuinely enjoyed their interactions with him and highly valued the positive relationship they had developed. Even if their properties had not sold, they were inclined to choose Tim again for their real estate needs due to the strong rapport and trust he had established with them.

With Tim recently joining my brokerage, I am optimistic that his exceptional client relation skills will have a positive impact on my newer agents. I hope that his ability to establish strong rapport and foster trust with clients will serve as an inspiration and example for them to enhance their own customer interactions. Having someone like Tim on board brings valuable expertise and a fresh perspective that can contribute to the growth and success of our team.

Similarly, at T-Mobile, I observed a coworker who possessed the ability to leverage her attractiveness and charisma to her advantage. By utilizing her charm, she could establish connections with customers, making them feel special and creating a sense of familiarity. This approach allowed her to tap into the emotions and desires of potential buyers, making them more likely to purchase a phone.

In the art of sales, leveraging one's unique skillset is crucial for success. While physical attributes are not a strength in my case, I recognized the importance of persistence and building strong relationships. Understanding the opportune moments to ask for the sale and not letting rejection deter me became key elements of my approach. I realized that sales is a continuous process that requires resilience and an unwavering determination to achieve positive outcomes. By honing these skills and maintaining a persistent mindset, I was able to overcome challenges and achieve success in my sales endeavors.

While certain weaknesses, such as my physical appearance, may be unchangeable, there are numerous skillsets that can be developed and improved upon. In the realm of sales, one of the greatest hurdles individuals face is the fear of rejection. The mere thought of receiving a "no" or upsetting someone can be daunting and lead to a fear of failure.

In the early days of YouTube, a gentleman named Jia Jiang embarked on a remarkable journey called the "100 Days of Rejection" challenge. Each day, he deliberately sought out situations where he knew he would face rejection. In one of his videos he requested a donut shop to create an intricate Olympic logo-shaped donut cake. This went viral, garnering over 5 million views. The remarkable part was that the donut shop employee went above and beyond to fulfill his request, leaving Jia astonished and even moved to tears.

From this experience, we can glean two valuable lessons. Firstly, when you treat people with kindness and respect, as exemplified by the donut shop employee, they are more inclined to support your endeavors and contribute to your success. Secondly, practice plays a vital role in overcoming the fear of rejection. By repeatedly facing rejection, you become more resilient and improve your ability to handle and learn from such experiences.

Embracing rejection as a learning opportunity and treating others with genuine care and appreciation are powerful principles that can positively impact your sales journey. With practice and a shift in perspective, you can navigate the fear of rejection and ultimately enhance your sales skills.

Mastering a skill takes time and practice; rarely does one create a masterpiece like the Mona Lisa on their first attempt. It applies to any profession, including sales, where continuous effort and improvement are necessary to excel. Trying different approaches, experimenting with different words, and becoming an expert in the art of selling are crucial steps towards success. The only way to truly develop these skills is to keep engaging in the sales process.

In the movie "American Underdog," an inspiring story unfolds around Kurt Warner, who receives a tryout with the Green Bay Packers right after college. Despite lacking knowledge of the playbook and feeling unprepared, Kurt's coach attempts to thrust him into practice. However, Kurt musters the courage to admit he isn't ready. Unfortunately, he gets cut from the team shortly afterward, leaving us wondering how things might have turned out if he had taken the leap anyway.

This anecdote emphasizes the importance of seizing opportunities and being willing to take risks. While preparation is crucial, sometimes, in the face of uncertainty, taking the leap and giving it your best shot can lead to unexpected outcomes. It underscores the need to strike a balance between readiness and embracing the challenges that come your way.

Just like Kurt Warner's experience, perseverance and a willingness to step out of your comfort zone are vital in the pursuit of success. Keep refining your craft, learn from each attempt, and embrace the journey of growth and self-improvement in the realm of sales.

Chapter 3: Setting goals

"You should set goals beyond your reach so you always have something to strive for" -Ted Turner

To be completely honest, even if just one individual reads this book and incorporates a positive change into their life, I consider it a victory. However, given my competitive and driven nature, I have set specific sales goals for the book. As you engage with this book, your personal objective should be to extract a handful of ideas and actively apply them to enhance your own life.

Without a doubt, I am an ardent advocate of setting goals. It goes without saying that I wouldn't embark on writing a book without a clear objective in mind. While it's undoubtedly gratifying to be able to proclaim oneself as an author, I aspire to take it a step further by sharing my specific goals for undertaking this literary endeavor. To me, if this book fails to reach a sales figure of 250 copies, I would consider it a personal setback that may dissuade me from pursuing future writing projects. On the other hand, if I manage to surpass the threshold of 250 copies sold, I will deem it a satisfactory achievement and likely be motivated to write another book. However, the pinnacle of triumph for me would be the sale of over 1,000 copies, which I would perceive as an exceptional triumph and cause for celebration. Thank you for purchasing and reading this book.

Setting goals is an essential aspect of achieving success in sales, as well as in any other area of life. Without clear goals, it becomes challenging to measure progress, stay motivated, and make focused efforts towards meaningful accomplishments. In this chapter, we will explore the importance of goal setting and provide practical strategies to help you establish and pursue your sales goals effectively.

Setting goals provides a clear target to aim for, ensuring that you navigate your path with purpose and precision. Without goals, you are akin to shooting at a target blindfolded, relying solely on luck for success. However, by setting goals, you enhance your chances of hitting the mark. Personally, I establish goals on an annual basis, as well as five-year goals and longer-term aspirations. Remarkably, every goal I set in my mid-20s to accomplish by the time I turned forty was triumphantly achieved before reaching thirty, resulting in the exhilarating need to recalibrate and set new goals. Such moments of accomplishment bring an indescribable sense of fulfillment and satisfaction.

Another objective I set for myself was to achieve a net worth of one million dollars by the age of forty, measured by the equity in my assets, I have surpassed that milestone. Despite initially appearing as an ambitious goal, I managed to accomplish it before reaching thirty years old. At present, my property portfolio boasts a net equity of nearly three million dollars, and that figure doesn't even account for the value of my businesses, my cash reserves (although not as substantial as desired), or my investments in cryptocurrency and stocks.

It is important to note that investing in real estate tends to be a business model that prioritizes long-term equity growth over immediate cash flow. Although there are strategies to generate cash flow in real estate, leveraging bank loans often results in minimal positive cash flow until the properties are fully paid off. Reflecting on my journey, if I were to start anew, I would allocate more funds into stocks and cryptocurrency earlier on. I continue to learn and adapt as I go, as financial education was not a domain my family was familiar with.

When I embarked on the journey of establishing Deacon Hoover Real Estate Advisors, my aim was to have a team of over twenty agents within five years. To my delight, when we reached the five-year milestone, last September, we had surpassed that target and had over forty-five agents on board. Presently, we have expanded even further and currently boast a team of fifty-five agents. While I may not have fully comprehended the challenges that awaited me when I started a real estate brokerage, I am incredibly satisfied with the progress and outcomes we have achieved thus far. One aspect that brings me immense joy is being able to assist my agents in realizing their financial aspirations.

In the previous year, we witnessed ten agents earning six-figure incomes, with a few of them even surpassing that threshold. This is especially noteworthy considering the relatively limited number of employment opportunities in our Pittsburgh area that offer such high earning potential. The median household income in our locality hovers just below fifty-five thousand dollars. As a non-franchised brokerage, we made a conscious decision to focus on nurturing new and underperforming agents, helping them evolve into top producers. While this endeavor presents its own set of challenges, the rewards are truly fulfilling.

Now that our reputation has been solidified, we have begun to attract more experienced agents to join our team. A prime example is Tim, whom I mentioned earlier, and who is now a valued member of our brokerage.

Goals can extend beyond professional endeavors, greatly impacting our personal lives as well. I firmly believe in the notion of striving to be the best version of ourselves each day. At the age of thirty, I had a significant wake-up call during a doctor's appointment. Weighing around 310 pounds, the doctor candidly informed me of the potential consequences of continuing down that path. His words were direct: "Mr. Hoover, if you continue on this trajectory, you will likely develop diabetes by the time you turn forty and face an untimely demise."

It took some time for me to process the gravity of that information, but I eventually decided to take action. Initially, I focused on increasing my physical activity, but I found that it had little impact on my weight. It wasn't until late 2019 when I set a specific goal to establish a healthy lifestyle. Importantly, I chose to embark on this journey before January 1, as I recognized the often fleeting nature of New Year's resolutions. As of writing this, I currently weigh 217 pounds. I firmly believe that without setting a goal, this transformation would never have taken place. I would still be struggling with excess weight and succumbing to unhealthy eating habits.

One of the key factors I identified was my diet. Educating myself about the nutritional content of the foods I consumed was a revelation. I also made the decision to eliminate craft beers from my routine, as they typically contain 200-400 calories per drink. Instead, I opted for healthier alternatives such as bourbon on the rocks or vodka soda, which are lower in caloric content. This change has made a significant difference in managing my weight.

As I continue to set and achieve goals, I have noticed a remarkable boost in confidence and the belief that I can accomplish nearly anything I set my mind to. I am confident that you, too, will experience this transformation once you embark on your own goal-setting journey.

Several business coaches I've worked with over the years have emphasized the importance of SMART goals. SMART stands for specific, measurable, achievable, relevant, and time-bound. Reflecting on the retail example from Chapter Two, let's consider setting a short-term goal for quickly advancing in that career. Here's an example of a SMART goal:

"My goal is to secure a commission-based position with a minimum earning potential of $50,000 per year. By the end of my first full year in this role, I aim to become the top-performing employee in my location. Furthermore, I strive to be promoted into a management position within two years of my employment."

This goal encompasses all the SMART criteria and could potentially be broken down into two or three separate goals. However, for the sake of this example, I've consolidated them into one comprehensive goal. To solidify this goal, it is essential to write or print it out and display it where you will encounter it daily, ideally multiple times throughout the day. Personally, I have my goals posted in prominent locations and also have them displayed on my phone's calendar twice per day, ensuring they are the first thing I see in the morning and the last thing before bed.

Expanding on the idea of goal posting, there is an insightful book called "Think and Grow Rich" by Napoleon Hill. Although it may be dry to read, Hill emphasizes the importance of affirming your goals by repeating them aloud twice a day. According to Hill, the act of saying and believing in your goals increases the likelihood of their manifestation. While the book may present some challenges during the reading process, it offers valuable concepts that can be applied to both your business and personal life. I strongly recommend giving it a read and exploring the ideas within.

One of the most crucial aspects of setting goals, as well as any endeavor in life, is eliminating excuses. Excuses have a negative impact, holding you back and undermining your goals at all costs. Your mind has a way of creating excuses to sabotage your progress and achievements. To counter this, it is essential to eradicate the word "can't" from your mindset and replace it with the phrase "How can I". This simple change in perspective can have a profound effect on your results.

Removing negativity from your life is vital for success. If you have negative friends or family members, it may be worth considering spending less time with them. As you embark on your journey towards success through the art of sales, you will encounter people who try to bring you down and convince you that your goals are impossible. They may claim to have your best interests at heart, but in reality, they may struggle to handle your success. Over the past decade, I have distanced myself from individuals who were once considered great friends or part of my family but revealed their true colors. Instead, I have surrounded myself with positive influences and supportive individuals. There is a saying that you are the average of the five people you spend the most time with. Take a close look at your circle and ask yourself if that is the kind of person you aspire to be.

Sometimes, adding just one person to your circle who embodies the qualities you desire can make a world of difference. To my surprise, many of my friends joined me on my journey because I had been a part of their circle. I am proud of them for making difficult decisions and accompanying me on this transformative journey.

Now that we've covered these important aspects, have you set your goals? Are you prepared? Establishing meaningful SMART goals and removing excuses from your mind is not only a valuable skill but also an excellent starting point.

"Lack of direction, not lack of time, is the problem. We all have twenty-four hour day" Zig Ziglar

Chapter 4: Relationship building

"Your most unhappy customers are your greatest source of learning" - Bill Gates

"There is only one boss. The customer. And he can fire everybody in the company from the chairman on down, simply by spending his money somewhere else" - Sam Walton

Mastering the skill of building relationships in sales can be challenging. Take, for example, selling a wireless phone to a customer who is shopping around. You have a limited window of ten to twenty minutes maximum to establish rapport, educate them about your product, differentiate yourself from the competition, and, most importantly, ask for the sale. If a salesperson is falling short of their goals, it often indicates a weakness in relationship building and a lack of consistent closing attempts.

To succeed, you must ask open-ended questions, actively listen, and gather as much information as possible during the brief interaction. Learn about their family, occupation, and hobbies. Your goal is to understand their needs and preferences thoroughly. For instance, in the wireless industry, if you neglect to inquire about their living arrangements, you may miss the opportunity to add additional lines for family members, or offer them a tablet instead. Discovering that they own a business opens up possibilities for providing internet services or supplying phones to their employees, highlighting the tax benefits associated with such arrangements.

Utilizing a CRM (Customer Relationship Management) system can greatly enhance this process. Imagine signing up a family for three lines, and one of their children is not yet old enough for a phone. By entering this information into your CRM and setting a reminder to contact them around the child's birthday, you can seize the opportunity to offer a thoughtful gift. This level of personalized service transforms you from being just a salesperson to an account manager dedicated to their satisfaction. Building these relationships goes beyond the transaction—it involves becoming their trusted advisor for all their future needs.

Maintaining contact outside of work is also valuable. As you transition from retail sales to your next endeavor, reaching out to clients and expressing your appreciation for their business can keep you top of mind. By nurturing these relationships, you may even find that many of your best repeat and referral customers become close friends. In a world where exceptional service is becoming increasingly rare, going the extra mile and treating each client as your only client will truly set you apart. Remember to connect on personal occasions like birthdays and holidays, and stay engaged by discussing shared interests or recent events. Following Gary Keller's "33 touch" system, which advocates contacting clients 33 times throughout the year, may initially seem excessive, but with a strong foundation of relationship building and detailed notes, you will always have meaningful topics to discuss.

Ultimately, investing in relationships and delivering exceptional service can have a profound impact on your success in sales. By treating each client as a valued individual, you can create lasting connections and stand out in a world where genuine care and attention are increasingly rare.

Recall those moments when you received exceptional service. Consider how it made you feel and the impression it left on you. This is the kind of experience you should strive to create for your clients. Your aim is to wow them with your outstanding service, and the information you gather during the sales process plays a vital role in achieving this. The more you know about your clients, the better equipped you are to go above and beyond their expectations.

Take a cue from large technology companies that prioritize data collection. They understand the immense value of knowing everything about their consumers, from their shopping preferences to their whereabouts. Why? Because they recognize the vast potential for success when armed with such knowledge. As sales professionals, we too should adopt a similar mindset. We must know our customers better than they know themselves. Become a valuable resource, a trusted friend, and an industry expert whom they rely on for all their needs.

By leveraging the information you gather and using it to personalize your approach, you can create an unparalleled level of service. Treat each client as a unique individual, anticipating their preferences and providing tailored solutions.

This level of attentiveness will not only leave a lasting impression but also position you as their go-to expert within your field. Strive to surpass their expectations, constantly finding ways to enhance their experience and deliver exceptional value.

Remember, exceptional service is not a one-time occurrence—it is a consistent commitment to understanding and meeting your clients' needs. By cultivating a deep understanding of your clients and going above and beyond to serve them, you can create a remarkable experience that sets you apart from the competition and fosters long-term loyalty.

Recently, I made a purchase for airfare to travel to New Orleans. Due to inconvenient flight schedules, I ended up booking two one-way flights with different airlines. However, a week before our trip, I realized that I had mistakenly booked the return flight from Pittsburgh instead of returning to Pittsburgh. Realizing my error, I immediately took action and visited southwest.com to rearrange my flight. Unfortunately, I discovered that changing my flight would cost twice the original amount. Unwilling to accept this, I decided to contact Southwest Airlines directly.

During my call, I explained the mistake I had made and asked if there were any alternatives or solutions available. The representative requested information about our availability for the return flight and placed me on hold for a brief period. Upon returning to the call, she informed me of the same information I already knew - changing the flight would indeed cost double the original amount. I inquired if there were any other options or if I could receive a refund to book elsewhere. According to their policy, changes for the type of ticket I had purchased needed to be made within 48 hours. However, she asked for a moment to consult with her supervisor.

After a short hold, the representative returned and surprised me by informing me that she had spoken with her supervisor. They agreed to match the previous rates for an undersold flight back to Pittsburgh. I was taken aback by this unexpected resolution! I expressed my gratitude multiple times, and I even asked if there was a way for me to leave a review for her outstanding service. Her response, however, was that I should simply go on my trip and have a fantastic time with my family.

If this representative had been local, I would have considered hiring her for something or, at the very least, consistently utilizing her services within her industry. This incident perfectly exemplifies the point I am trying to make. As a result of the exceptional service I received, my perception of Southwest has greatly improved. I am now a loyal Southwest fan, and I intend to spend more money with them in the future due to the remarkable service provided by this representative.

One of the major mistakes I made during my time in the wireless industry was not retaining all of my customer data. While I kept the information of those clients whom I knew would bring future sales, I neglected to keep the details of others. Throughout my tenure at T-Mobile USA, I sold to over 5,000 clients (oh, how I wish they had a residual commission plan!). If I had maintained the data of all these customers, I would have begun my real estate sales career with a potential client base of 5,000 individuals, all of whom I had previously worked with in my earlier profession. It would have been like adding fuel to a fire, and I have no doubt that I would have sold more properties as a result.

Although T-Mobile may not have approved of this practice, there was nothing they could have done to prevent it. As the primary point of contact for the company, I had the right to retain their information. Even if I had converted those 5,000 contacts at an extremely low rate, let's say just two percent, it would still mean that I missed out on 100 sales. Not to mention, if I had done an excellent job with those 100 sales, I would have gained even more business through referrals from their friends and family. This mistake likely cost me somewhere in the range of half a million dollars. Consider this: If the average sales price in our area was $150,000 at the time, and my commission was three percent, that would amount to $4,500 per transaction. Multiply that by 100 transactions (representing 2% of the 5,000 clients), and the total would be $450,000. And that's not even taking into account referrals and future home purchases—just the initial transactions alone. It's mind-boggling to think about. If you ever doubted the importance of relationship building as a crucial skillset, I hope this serves as a convincing example.

Leave a lasting impact on every person you encounter in life, and make sure to follow up with them regularly, making them feel special. It's not rocket science, but if it were, I wouldn't excel at it.

The purpose of this book is to provide you with the fundamental knowledge to enhance your life through the art of selling. My intention is for this book to benefit you not only in your professional and financial endeavors but also on a personal level. In just a few concise chapters, I have already shared how these skills have enabled me to advance in my careers, secure my financial future, and improve my overall well-being.

I strongly encourage you to explore these skills more deeply throughout your career and life journey. A highly recommended book in the realm of building relationships is "How to Win Friends and Influence People" by Dale Carnegie. It is an exceptional read that primarily focuses on the art of cultivating relationships. I personally have found great value in revisiting it multiple times.

What is truly remarkable about the world we live in is that, for a minimal cost of acquiring a book, you can learn from the very best. This allows you to continually improve yourself and take one step closer towards becoming the best in your chosen career path.

"You can make more friends in two months by becoming interested in other people than you can in two years trying to get other people interested in you" -Dale Carnegie

If we reflect on the concepts discussed in Chapter One, which emphasized the importance of taking action, it becomes evident that enhancing our relationship-building skills is an area we can begin improving immediately. This applies not only to our interactions with friends and family but also extends to our romantic relationships (an aspect I personally should have dedicated more attention to) and prospective employers. The opportunities to implement these skills are abundant in various aspects of our lives.

Let us remember that we were born with two ears and only one mouth, signifying the significance of listening more than speaking. When we do engage in conversation, our focus should be on inquiring about the other person, rather than solely expressing our own views. By adopting this approach, we can foster stronger relationships. It is important to shift our attention away from our own perspectives and genuinely listen to the thoughts and feelings of others. While we may never attain perfection in this regard, we can certainly make strides toward improvement.

Chapter 5: Negotiation

"Information is a negotiator's greatest weapon" - Victor Kiam

"In business you don't get what you deserve, you get what you negotiate" - Jay-Z

I have a deep passion for the art of negotiation, and in this chapter, I am excited to share valuable insights and tips that will prove indispensable in your future endeavors. Negotiation skills will undoubtedly play a significant role in various aspects of your life, and I am eager to provide real-world examples of how I have effectively negotiated both in business and personal contexts.

If you have yet to explore the DISC assessment system, I highly recommend delving into it. This system enables individuals to determine their personality type, along with their unique strengths and weaknesses. By gaining a deeper understanding of oneself and others, particularly in terms of personality traits, you can enhance your ability to read people and effectively negotiate. Knowing the strengths and weaknesses of the individuals you negotiate with can greatly facilitate the negotiation process.

Mastering the art of persuasion and negotiation has the potential to yield substantial financial gains and savings throughout your lifetime. Therefore, it is crucial to develop and refine these skills to achieve success in your negotiations.

An excellent resource for delving deeper into the subject of negotiation is the book "Never Split the Difference" by Chris Voss. While I may not fully align with the title, I frequently employ a technique similar to splitting the difference. However, I strategically utilize this approach later in the negotiation process compared to most people. Typically, I wait until it seems that both parties have reached their maximum limits before introducing the split the difference tactic. For instance, I might say, "While I do not believe my client can go any higher, what if I could get him to meet in the middle? Would that be acceptable to your client?" This technique often yields a high success rate, as the other party agrees or reveals their lowest or highest limit in the negotiation. While most of the time my clients are willing to accept the current offer on the table, I still aim to push for more since the price is unlikely to change.

Some individuals argue that an offer is only good if it is somewhat insulting. However, our goal in negotiation is to secure the best possible price without alienating the other party. A poorly worded statement can easily backfire, resulting in the loss of even the existing acceptable deal on the table. Ultimately, our objective is to win negotiations by obtaining the best deal available while maintaining positive relationships. Although burning bridges occasionally happens, it can also lead to new opportunities.

As an example, a few years into my real estate sales career, I represented a client purchasing an apartment building that included a parking lot behind it, as advertised. During negotiations, my client asked about the most cost-effective way to acquire the lot along with the building. Prior to the negotiation, I followed my usual practice of researching the person I was negotiating with. In this case, I discovered that the agent on the other side was relatively new to the field and faced language barriers. Familiarity with laws and regulations also played a role.

In Pennsylvania, lots are not considered "posted" addresses, allowing us to include the parcel number in the contract without mentioning the additional address. Based on my research, I advised my client to simply add the parcel number to the agreement, assuming that the other party might not thoroughly review the contract, thereby giving us the lot at no additional cost. The offer was accepted, and during the inspection period, the seller was surprised when my client expressed disinterest in the lot. To clarify, my client calmly told the seller to "check the agreement." The seller became upset with his agent for missing the provision, and to appease him, my client agreed to pay him a reduced amount of two thousand dollars for the lot. Additionally, the seller convinced the listing agent to waive her commission due to the mistake. Interestingly, the listing agent did not attend the closing, expressing her dissatisfaction with not being compensated. The seller, impressed by my client's handling of the situation, asked for my business card, stating his intention to work with a more competent agent in the future. While I could have been more forthright with the agent about the provision, my ultimate responsibility as a fiduciary is to my client's best interests. It was the agent's responsibility to thoroughly read the contract she was having her client sign.

I would not have been able to secure such a favorable deal for my client without conducting thorough research, understanding the property, being knowledgeable about the laws and processes, empathizing with the other party's perspective, and having the confidence to take action. A more experienced agent would have likely caught the provision during the contract review and criticized my approach. However, I was dealing with a relatively inexperienced agent who had limited sales experience and faced language barriers. While I am unsure if she is still in the real estate business, one thing is certain: if she is, she undoubtedly learned a valuable lesson through this transaction. Our professional relationship may be strained or even severed, as she may not willingly choose to work with me again. Nevertheless, the bridge burned with her opens up new opportunities for me, as her client is now my client. Ultimately, my primary objective is to serve my clients to the best of my abilities, and in this case, I successfully achieved that goal.

Assuming the sale is a crucial aspect of effective negotiation. During my time at T-Mobile USA, I consistently achieved impressive overall numbers across various metrics, including phone sales, activations, upgrades, features, accessories, insurance, and average rate plan premiums, among others. Unlike many other representatives who struggled to meet the minimum accessory sales expectations, I never encountered such difficulties.

One of my preferred techniques for selling accessories was to assume the sale. By diligently cultivating a strong rapport with my clients, they had come to know, like, and trust me (as referenced in BNI). When it was time for them to pay for their phone, I would take a moment to gather all the relevant accessories from around the store, such as Bluetooth headsets, cases, screen protectors, stylists, extra batteries, and car chargers—essentially any accessory available. I would then ring up the total cost of the phone along with all the accessories, stating, "Your total today for the phone and all the available accessories is $XXX.XX."

At this point, the clients would typically examine the accessories and occasionally express that they didn't require a particular item among the five to ten accessories on the counter. However, it was quite rare for someone to outright decline all the accessories. They hesitated to do so after experiencing the exceptional treatment and care I had provided throughout the transaction. Our target at the time was to sell $30 worth of accessories for every phone sold (back when cases were priced at $15, not $75), but it was not uncommon for me to exceed this goal by 2-3 times.

Nevertheless, it is important to read the client and assess the situation. If you haven't established a solid rapport or the atmosphere doesn't feel conducive, it may be more appropriate to present all the available accessories and explain their value and significance, rather than assuming the sale. With practice and attentiveness to different scenarios, you will learn the appropriate approach to negotiations and become a more refined negotiator. It's essential to learn from any mistakes you make along the way in order to enhance your negotiation skills.

By the way, BNI stands for Business Networking International. If you are in a commission-based role with a flexible schedule, it might be worth considering joining BNI. Essentially, it is a business referral organization where a group of ten to one hundred individuals gather once a week to exchange ideas and refer clients to one another. What sets BNI apart is its category exclusivity, meaning that if you join as a mortgage company, you will be the only representative from that industry within the group.

Over the years, I have developed meaningful friendships through BNI and found it to have a significant impact on my businesses. It provides a valuable platform for networking and building connections, which can be highly advantageous in a commission-based profession.

Let's discuss the personal negotiation process when it comes to car shopping. While some individuals may consider tax benefits, most people approach car shopping for personal reasons. While some may despise the process, I find enjoyment in it. The first step is conducting thorough research on the vehicle you intend to purchase, including identifying dealers, determining the best times to buy, understanding average prices, and exploring financing options.

In the automotive industry, the last three days of the month are often considered the optimal time to buy a car. During this period, sales managers are motivated to maintain their positions or earn additional incentives, making it an ideal opportunity for negotiation. Typically, I begin by test driving various vehicles early in the month to narrow down my choices. Then, I identify the top three dealerships offering competitive prices and ensure the desired vehicles are in stock.

Around the third week of the month, I initiate the negotiation process. I visit each dealer, provide my contact information, specify my requirements, and listen to their pitches. I inform them that I will be making a purchase within the next week or two, emphasizing my intention to explore other options as well. Prior to the last three days of the month, the dealers will likely reach out to me, eager to secure my business. This is when the real negotiation begins. I inform them that their competitors are offering certain deals, and I inquire about what they can offer me. I also mention that I have excellent credit and available cash if necessary. I clearly communicate whether I plan to lease or buy and state the desired terms, expressing interest in specific finance deals advertised by the manufacturer.

In the case of my most recent car purchase, a Jaguar F-type, a high-end sports car, by the second-to-last day of the month, all three sales managers were emailing me, expressing their interest in earning my business. At this point, I would send them cost sheets from their direct competitors. By the last day of the month, I had eliminated one dealer, and the remaining two were closely matched in terms of price. Through negotiation, I managed to secure a discount of approximately

$7,000 on the vehicle, with both dealers offering additional protections for the car.

Another important aspect of negotiation is being aware of available extra features in advance. Luxury vehicles often provide VIP add-ons, such as vehicle pickup for service and loaner cars, as well as essential features like gap insurance. Gap insurance covers the difference between the insurance payout and the remaining amount owed on the vehicle in case of an accident. The winning dealer in my case included the VIP package and gap insurance as part of the deal, but with the condition that I made the purchase on the last day of the month. The VIP package alone was valued at $2,500, and the gap insurance was an additional $2,000. In total, I saved nearly $12,000, which amounted to around 10% off the sticker price of the car.

Taking a broader perspective on this negotiation, let's consider the long-term impact. If I were to purchase a new vehicle every five years from the age of 18 to 70 (for simplicity, let's assume I only own one vehicle at a time), that would amount to ten vehicles over my lifetime. If I were to save an average of ten thousand dollars on each purchase compared to the typical consumer, this negotiation strategy would result in a total savings of one hundred thousand dollars over my lifetime. It is important to note that this calculation only accounts for one individual vehicle purchase at a time and doesn't factor in negotiations on trade allowances.

While many people may not approach car buying with this long-term perspective, it's worth mentioning that technology, such as online ordering and the rise of companies like Tesla, may disrupt traditional negotiations in the future. However, the key point here is that negotiation skills can be applied to almost every aspect of life. Negotiations occur daily, whether deciding where to eat dinner, choosing what to have for dinner, or even negotiating with my children on various matters. Even intimate relationships with our spouses involve negotiation. By focusing on improving our negotiation skills, we can enhance all aspects of our lives.

A crucial aspect of the vehicle purchase example is that I was in a fortunate position where I didn't necessarily need to buy a vehicle. I already had a reliable vehicle, so if I couldn't secure a favorable deal, I could continue searching. This highlights an essential element of negotiation: leverage. By avoiding the situation where you desperately need something, you maintain the upper hand in negotiations.

"Leverage is the reason some people become rich and others do not become rich" -Robery Kiyosaki

According to the dictionary, leverage refers to using something to maximum advantage. In negotiations, the party with more favorable circumstances holds the upper hand. Over the past few years, the real estate industry has experienced an unprecedented seller's market due to various factors such as low inventory, low interest rates, and shifting housing needs. Sellers have gained significant advantage, selling their homes well above market value without much room for buyer negotiation. Witnessing this one-sided and highly competitive market has dampened the excitement of negotiating a home purchase or sale for me personally. Even on the listing side, it becomes a monotonous process of reviewing multiple offers and asking buyers for their best offer. This market situation highlights the importance of leverage in negotiation. I anticipate that the market will eventually undergo a 180-degree shift, favoring buyers once again. As an investor, this will present great opportunities to purchase properties. However, many homeowners may find themselves with negative equity, having paid inflated prices for their homes.

It serves as a reminder that negotiation should be a constant consideration in every transaction we encounter. Whether it's saving money on bills by threatening to terminate services or battling with service providers for fair treatment, leveraging the threat of termination often reveals better offers. I experienced this first hand in my yearly negotiations with DirecTV, where I discovered that a simple call to cancel resulted in a special representative authorized to offer more reasonable costs to retain me as a customer. These companies understand the value of customer retention and are willing to make special offers to keep existing customers. Time is a valuable resource, and dedicating some of it to negotiating bills instead of indulging in leisure activities can lead to significant savings and skill development in negotiation.

Developing expertise as a professional negotiator is an invaluable skill that can yield significant benefits. It requires dedication to honing your abilities by investing time and effort. Embrace every opportunity to practice negotiation, and actively seek out additional chances to sharpen your skills. Proficiency in negotiation will not only boost your earnings in commission-based sales roles but also enable you to save money by effectively negotiating bills and purchases. Moreover, these skills can extend beyond professional settings and positively impact various aspects of your personal life. Remember to maintain leverage throughout the negotiation process, ensuring you hold as many advantageous positions as possible. Thoroughly study the product or service, analyze the competition, and identify optimal times for negotiation. By doing so, you'll enhance your abilities and increase your chances of achieving successful outcomes.

Chapter 6: Objections

"An objection is not a rejection, it is simply a request for more information" -Bo Bennett

Objections, although often viewed negatively in sales, are an inherent part of the sales process. The quote above encapsulates it perfectly: when a prospect raises an objection, they are essentially seeking more information. As sales professionals, it is our responsibility to recognize this and respond accordingly. Instead of being discouraged, we should take a step back, ask open-ended questions, and determine the most effective way to provide the necessary information to close the sale. Frequently, several objections need to be overcome before reaching a successful outcome.

In industries like real estate, where the process can span weeks or even months, numerous objections and obstacles must be addressed along the way. Whenever my agents express frustration over objections or obstacles, I remind them that if it were easy, consumers would undertake the task themselves and forego the expertise we offer. In this chapter, I will explore some of the most common objections I have encountered repeatedly and discuss respectful and dignified strategies for overcoming them. There are abundant resources available on this subject, and I particularly enjoy watching

YouTube videos as they often provide fresh perspectives and novel ideas that I can borrow. After all, the best ideas are often inspired by others.

Objection 1: "Just looking / not interested" - When faced with this objection from an inbound lead, the common response is to say, "Let me know if things change." However, a more effective approach is to ask an open-ended question. To illustrate this, I will draw from my current and past professions.

Recruiting agents is a significant part of my current sales efforts. Recently, an agent reached out to me seeking a solution for a problem he was facing. The first step was to attentively listen to his issue and provide guidance on how to overcome it. Once we resolved the problem, I asked about the state of his business, fully aware that most agents are struggling to close deals at present. He responded, "It's a bit light, but we are powering through." Sensing his lukewarm sentiment towards his current company, I inquired about his satisfaction with his current position. He expressed that it was merely okay. This response indicated that he was not particularly satisfied with his current company. Seizing the opportunity, I suggested meeting up for lunch or coffee to further discuss his situation. Meeting in person is often a crucial step in initiating a sales call. Consequently, he agreed to schedule a lunch appointment with me for next week. Now, all that remains is to successfully close the deal when we meet face-to-face. More insights on closing techniques will be covered in a later chapter of this book.

In the context of outbound sales, the dynamics are indeed different. When reaching out to potential customers proactively, you need to identify their needs and demonstrate why your product or service would be valuable to them. Let us delve into a similar outbound situation.

Unlike inbound leads where prospects have already expressed interest, in outbound sales I must effectively convey the benefits and demonstrate why they should consider my offering. By understanding their unique situation and aligning my product's features and benefits with their specific needs, I increase the chances of piquing their interest and ultimately closing the sale.

In outbound sales, it is crucial to initiate conversations with a clear understanding of the customer's needs and be able to articulate how your product or service can provide a solution. By effectively conveying the value proposition and addressing their pain points, you can engage potential customers and generate interest even when they may not have been actively seeking your product or service.

Consider a scenario where the agent didn't reach out to me, but I have identified them as a potential fit for our company based on their declining sales. To initiate contact, I would make a call and introduce myself in the following manner: "Hello Agent, my name is Ian Hoover, and I am the broker owner of Deacon Hoover Real Estate. Do you have a moment to speak?"

By starting the conversation with a brief introduction and asking if it is a good time to talk, I avoid pushing forward if they indicate that it is not a suitable moment. If they object or express inconvenience, I simply inquire, "What would be a good time for us to chat?" This way, I maintain a level of curiosity without revealing the specific reason for my call. The agent may assume I have an issue with them or one of my agents.

If the agent inquires about the purpose of my call, I respond with, "Yes, but would now be a good time to talk?" It is important not to reveal my cards until the right moment. Once I determine this is an appropriate time to discuss further, I proceed with the reason for my call. For example, I might say, "Mr. Agent, I've been closely monitoring the market, and I've noticed that your sales have experienced a 30% decline year over year. I understand there are challenges, but I'm curious to hear your thoughts on this."

Even at this point, I haven't fully disclosed my intentions to the agent. They may believe I'm seeking their opinion. I would follow up with, "I see. I was hoping we could meet next week to discuss our industry. Are you available for lunch on Monday or Wednesday?" There is the possibility that I may encounter an objection at this stage.

To address any objections, I respond simply with, "My focus is to help agents improve their business, and it is a more involved conversation. Does Monday or Wednesday work better for you?" If they continue to object, I emphasize that I will be treating them to lunch at a restaurant of their choice and express confidence that the meeting will provide valuable insights to enhance their business. I might share success stories from our agents, such as, "Lindsay from my firm initially had similar objections to meeting with me. However, with my assistance, she saw a remarkable 125% improvement in her business last year. Even a 50% increase in your production, given your current levels, could mean an extra $XX,XXX.XX in your pocket. I genuinely believe our meeting will be well worth fitting into your busy schedule. So, would Monday or Wednesday be more suitable?"

As you can see, I gradually provide more information while continuously asking for their commitment to the meeting. In this case, the "sale" for me is securing an in-person meeting.

In sales training courses, this process is commonly referred to as the "rule of three." It implies that you may encounter three rejections before obtaining a "yes." While there may be occasional easy sales where you receive an immediate "yes," more often than not, you will need to make two to four sales attempts before successfully closing the deal. Even the most skilled sales associates don't achieve a 100% closure rate.

If you're unable to close the deal (which is normal), this is where the persistent follow-up, which I discussed earlier in this book, becomes crucial. Just because the deal didn't close doesn't mean it is completely lost. It is important to continue following up, nurturing the relationship, and demonstrating the value of doing business with you. The only instance where I consider a lead to be "dead" is if they explicitly request to stop being contacted.

One of the most enjoyable inside sales experiences I have had was during my time in retail sales. It felt like shooting fish in a barrel, as there were a few objections we encountered daily. One common objection was when customers would say, "I'm just looking," which essentially meant they wanted to be left alone. However, as commission-based salespeople, we couldn't accept that. Overcoming this objection was relatively easy. We would start by building a relationship with the customer. If they were wearing something we could relate to, such as a sports team logo, we would comment on it. If there was nothing physical to connect with, we would focus on what they were looking at, saying something like, "That Samsung Galaxy Fold is pretty amazing. What phone are you currently using?" Although not as open-ended a question as I typically recommend, it would initiate conversation. When a customer entered my store saying they were just looking, they were essentially giving me permission to engage with them. If the salesperson failed to take advantage of that opportunity, it was their own fault for not closing the deal.

Another objection I encountered frequently was when customers would say, "I have to talk to the boss," referring to their spouse. This objection was more challenging to handle. In retail, an effective approach was to emphasize our two-week return and exchange policy with zero restocking fees. We would encourage customers to try the product for a test run, assuring them that they would love it. While this approach sometimes resulted in higher returns, it was a way to close the deal. Another tactic was to have the customer call their spouse while they were still in the store, putting them on speakerphone to involve them in the conversation and build rapport over the phone. Creating a sense of urgency was crucial in these situations, whether it was highlighting a limited-time sales promotion or emphasizing low inventory. Sometimes, being honest about needing to meet a monthly quota could also motivate the customer to make a decision. You have to gauge each client and try different approaches since some individuals require more time to think before making a decision. This is where follow-up comes into play.

The last objection I frequently heard was related to cost, with customers saying, "I can't afford it." This objection is unique because, at that point, we often don't know their specific financial situation. However, we can gather more information by inquiring about what they can't afford. For example, we might ask, "Is it the monthly bill or the termination fee from your old provider that you can't afford?" Once we narrow down their concern, we can craft a response tailored to address it. For instance, we might acknowledge the expensive termination fee but remind them that they mentioned earlier that our plan would save them $50 per month. We would explain that within four billing cycles, the savings would offset the termination fee, and they would continue saving money each month. Additionally, we could mention that they could sell or trade in their current phone to offset some or all of the cost. By addressing their objection and presenting multiple reasons why purchasing our product was a wise decision, we could help them make an informed choice.

Closing every single deal may not be realistic, but the key to improving your closing efficiency lies in being proactive and assertive. The distinction between an average salesperson and an exceptional one lies in their persistence, resilience, and unwavering drive. A great salesperson avoids allowing personal issues or workplace drama to affect their performance. They prioritize sales over distractions, leaving external factors at the door. While everyone may have an off day, the truly outstanding individuals still accomplish more on their worst days than the average ones do on their best. It's a mindset fueled by passion and a relentless desire to excel in their craft.

Consider the example of Michael Jordan, who didn't dwell on a bad game but instead practiced and mentally focused for the next one. He had the ability to have short-term memory loss and move on. Professional athletes, despite experiencing severe injuries, often return to the field with unwavering determination. Drew Bledsoe, Alex Smith, and Damar Hamlin, for instance, do not dwell on the fact that they could have died; they forget about it and focus on being professional athletes.

As salespeople, we must bring our A-game every day. This is our field of play, our livelihood, our reputation is at stake. If you aspire to be successful in sales but lack this mindset, it is essential to cultivate it. It is rare to find someone with a lackluster drive who achieves tremendous success. Among the truly successful individuals I know, they never stop. They embody their profession, dedicating themselves wholeheartedly to their work.

In the case of an expired listing call, overcoming the initial challenges of reaching homeowners who may not be aware that their property is no longer active on the market is important. They might not recognize you or even realize that their listing has expired. Despite these obstacles, your goal is to secure an appointment. Here is an example of how to approach the conversation:

"Hello, I was calling about your property at 123 Main St. Is it still available?"

Once they confirm, you introduce yourself and your company, and explain the purpose of your call:

"Great, my name is Ian Hoover, and I represent Deacon Hoover Real Estate. I wanted to reach out because I noticed that your property is no longer active on the market due to your listing contract expiring. I would love the opportunity to earn your business. I have Friday evening or Saturday morning available to meet with you and tour your home. Which works best for you?"

By addressing the main issue and offering to visit their property, you have already made progress in the conversation. However, you may encounter objections at this point, such as "We already have an agent." In response, you need to deliver a compelling message that grabs their attention:

"Actually, you are no longer under contract with your previous agent, and frankly, they failed to deliver the results you were looking for. Meeting with me carries no obligation. My firm has a proven track record of successfully selling expired listings. Would Friday evening or Saturday morning work better for you?"

If you don't have a personal track record, leverage your firm's track record in your pitch. However, if you do have a proven track record, you can highlight your own achievements in addition to your firm's reputation. Here's an adjusted version of the previous response:

"Actually, you are no longer under contract with your previous agent, and frankly, they failed to deliver the results you were looking for. Meeting with me carries no obligation. I have personally helped numerous homeowners like you successfully sell their expired listings, and my firm, Deacon Hoover Real Estate, has an outstanding track record as well. We are dedicated to achieving results. Would Friday evening or Saturday morning work better for you?"

By showcasing your personal expertise and mentioning your firm's strong track record, you provide additional reasons for the homeowners to choose you as their agent. It is essential to emphasize your credibility and the potential benefits they will receive by working with you and your reputable company.

By boldly stating that their previous agent did not meet their expectations, you demonstrate your confidence and determination. This is a powerful response to objections and shows that you mean business. Expect to encounter additional objections before they agree to meet with you, but remember that persistence is key to securing the in-person meeting.

Keeping a log of objections, especially the ones you struggle to overcome, can be a valuable practice. This log will help you analyze and refine your responses for future encounters. By focusing on areas where you fell short, you can continuously improve and handle objections more effectively in the future.

While some may choose to unwind and relax after work, dedicating your time to improving your skills sets you apart as a committed professional. Instead of spending your evenings watching Netflix or engaging in leisure activities, you choose to invest that time in personal and professional development. Whether reading books, attending training sessions, practicing sales techniques, or studying industry trends, your commitment to continuous improvement is commendable.

By consistently sharpening your skills, you position yourself for success. You gain a deeper understanding of your profession, acquire new knowledge and strategies, and stay updated on the latest trends and developments. This ongoing investment in self-improvement allows you to better serve your clients, overcome challenges, and ultimately achieve your goals.

Remember, the extra effort you put into improving your skills today will pay off in the long run. Embrace a mindset of continuous learning and growth, and use your time wisely to become a top-notch sales professional.

Understanding and effectively addressing objections is crucial in any profession. It's important to study and familiarize yourself with the potential objections specific to your industry. Take the time to develop well-crafted responses and strategies for each objection. Keeping a log or notes on objections you encounter, along with what works and what doesn't, will help you refine your approach over time.

In situations where you are unable to overcome a particular objection, seeking advice from others can be beneficial. Cultivating relationships with top salespeople within your company can provide valuable insights. Reach out to them when you encounter a challenging objection and ask for their advice. Alternatively, if your organization has sales reports available, you can consult them to identify the top performers in selling a specific product. Approach these successful individuals, offer to buy them a cup of coffee or a beer, and ask for their strategies or tips.

Surrounding yourself with high-performing individuals can positively influence your own performance. Building relationships with top producers within your organization can provide you with valuable guidance and insights to help you excel in your profession.

Chapter 7: Sales scripts

"Every sale has five obstacles; no need, no money, no desire, no trust" - Zig Ziglar

In any profession, having the right tools is essential for success. For a salesperson, one of the most valuable tools is a well-crafted script. Particularly for those starting out or looking to refine their skills, a script provides structure, guidance, and reminders of key talking points throughout the sales process.

A good script keeps you on track, ensuring that you cover all the necessary information and address potential objections. It serves as a roadmap, helping you navigate the conversation and steer it towards a desired outcome. With practice, you'll become more comfortable and proficient, eventually internalizing the script and adapting it to your own style.

It's important to note that while scripts are valuable, they should also allow room for personalization and authenticity. You can start with existing scripts available online and modify them to fit your specific industry, target audience, and personal approach. As you gain experience and learn what works best for you, don't hesitate to make adjustments and tailor the script to your own voice and style.

Different situations in sales require different scripts. For example, a real estate agent may need scripts for expired listings, for-sale-by-owner properties, internet leads, cold calls, and off-market opportunities. Each script should address the unique challenges and objectives associated with that particular situation.

Ultimately, the goal is to develop a repertoire of effective scripts that align with your sales objectives and resonate with your prospects. Over time, with practice and refinement, you'll become a confident and skilled sales professional who can adapt and engage in conversations fluidly, even without relying heavily on a script.

Practicing your script is crucial to deliver it with confidence and professionalism. The goal is to sound natural and authentic, while also conveying expertise and trustworthiness. Here are some key reasons why practicing your script is important:

1. Familiarity: By practicing your script repeatedly, you become familiar with the content, flow, and structure. This helps you internalize the information, making it easier to recall during conversations. As a result, you'll be more confident and fluent in delivering your message.

2. Smooth Delivery: Practicing your script helps you refine your delivery, ensuring a smooth and polished presentation. You can work on pacing, intonation, and emphasis to create a dynamic and engaging conversation. This avoids sounding

monotonous or robotic, which can turn off potential customers.

3. Overcoming Objections: Through practice, you become well-versed in addressing common objections and concerns that may arise during sales conversations. This allows you to respond confidently and provide persuasive counterpoints. Practicing objection handling helps you build trust and credibility with prospects.

4. Active Listening: When you're familiar with your script, you can focus more on actively listening to your prospect's responses and adapting your approach accordingly. Instead of struggling to remember what to say next, you can genuinely engage in the conversation and build rapport.

5. Confidence and Trust: Practicing your script instills confidence in your abilities and knowledge. When you confidently deliver your message, prospects perceive you as a professional who knows their stuff. This helps establish trust and credibility, crucial factors in building successful sales relationships.

Remember, practicing your script is not about memorizing it word for word. It's about understanding the key points, internalizing the flow and structure, and adapting it to fit your own style and personality. Regular practice will enhance your communication skills, boost your confidence, and make you a more effective salesperson.

Here is my expired listing script:

Hello [First Name],

I noticed that your home is no longer on the market, and I wanted to reach out to see if you're still interested in selling.

If Yes: Great! My name is [Your Name], and I'm with Deacon & Hoover Real Estate Advisors. Our brokerage has a proven track record of successfully selling homes that other agents have struggled with. We achieve this through honest assessments of the property and implementing strategic, aggressive marketing and pricing strategies.

I'd love to meet with you this week to discuss your home and develop a customized plan to get it sold. I have availability on Friday between 2 and 4 or Saturday between 10 and 12. Which of these times works best for you? I will give you a call the day of the appointment to confirm.

If No: I understand. In that case, are you planning to rent the home or live in it?

If Yes, renting: That's a great option as well. We have a sister company that specializes in property management, and we can assist you with various aspects of being a landlord. Let's meet this week to tour the home and discuss what needs to be done to make it rent compliant. I have availability from 3 to 5 on Friday or 10 to 12 on Saturday. Which of these time slots works better for you?

This initial meeting will provide you with valuable insights, and if you decide to rent, you'll earn a small commission while also gaining insider knowledge about the best time to sell in the future.

If you're unable to reach the homeowner by phone, you have a few options:

1. Send a letter: Mail them a personalized letter explaining the same information you would have discussed on the phone. Include your business card for easy contact.

2. In-person introduction: If you're in the vicinity, consider stopping by to introduce yourself in person. This personal touch can leave a lasting impression and open the door for further conversation.

The script mentioned above contains a few crucial elements. One of the most significant aspects is addressing the prospect by their first name at the beginning of the call. Rather than using formal titles like "Mr. Smith," using a friendly greeting like "Hi Tom!" creates a sense of familiarity. This approach makes the prospect feel like they already know you, helping to lower their guard and create a more comfortable atmosphere. In contrast, using formal titles can give the impression of a typical sales call, which may put the prospect on high alert.

Another essential component is the initial sales pitch that highlights the brokerage's track record in selling homes other agents have struggled with. This concise and direct message communicates the brokerage's expertise and specialization in addressing the prospect's specific situation. By focusing on their unique niche, the script establishes credibility and demonstrates the ability to provide a solution tailored to the prospect's needs.

It Is important to note that while this is not a real estate sales book, the script described above has proven to be highly effective and has generated substantial income over the years. It can be adapted and customized to fit various sales pitches or multiple sales scenarios. The key lies in modifying it to align with your individual sales approach and making it relevant to your specific industry and target audience.

Business-to-business outbound sales requires a distinct script, as doctors' offices often have front-line employees who screen incoming calls. Interestingly, I considered pursuing this career path before entering the real estate industry. Among the most financially rewarding sales positions, the top four include realtors, pharmaceutical sales representatives, enterprise sales professionals, and medical device sales representatives. It's worth noting that sales experience is typically required to secure a position in these highly lucrative sales roles.

Here's an example of a sales script for a pharmaceutical sales representative calling a doctor's office:

Introduction:
Hello, may I speak with Dr. [Doctor's Last Name], please?

Receptionist:

Yes, this is Dr. [Doctor's Last Name]'s office. May I ask who's calling?

Introduction:
Of course, my name is [Your Name], and I'm a pharmaceutical sales representative with [Company Name]. I specialize in [specific area or medication]. I wanted to briefly discuss a new treatment option that could benefit Dr. [Doctor's Last Name] and their patients.

Receptionist:
I can connect you with our office manager. Please hold on.

Transition:
Thank you. I appreciate it.

Office Manager/Assistant:
Hello, this is [Office Manager/Assistant Name]. How can I assist you?

Introduction:
Hi [Office Manager/Assistant Name]. This is [Your Name] from [Company Name]. I hope you're having a great day. I was hoping to speak with Dr. [Doctor's Last Name] about an innovative treatment option we have available.

Office Manager/Assistant:
Sure, let me see if the doctor is available. May I ask what it's regarding?

Value Proposition:

Absolutely. We have recently introduced [Medication/Product Name], which has shown remarkable success in treating [specific medical condition or symptom]. It offers [key benefits/features], and many doctors have seen significant improvement in their patients' quality of life.

Handling Objections (If Office Manager/Assistant shows hesitation):

I understand that Dr. [Doctor's Last Name] is busy, but I believe this treatment option could greatly benefit their patients. Our company has invested significant resources into developing this medication, and we are confident in its effectiveness. I would be more than happy to provide more information or schedule a brief appointment to discuss it further at their convenience.

Appointment Request:

If possible, I would appreciate it if you could help me schedule a meeting with Dr. [Doctor's Last Name] to discuss [Medication/Product Name] in more detail. I am available at [suggested date and time], but I am also flexible to work around the doctor's schedule.

Closing:

Thank you for your assistance, [Office Manager/Assistant Name]. I truly believe this treatment option can make a positive impact in your patients' lives, and I look forward to speaking with Dr. [Doctor's Last Name]. Please let me know the best way to coordinate our meeting.

Follow-up:

If I don't hear back within the next few days, I'll reach out again to ensure Dr. [Doctor's Last Name] receives the information. Thank you again for your time and have a wonderful day.

Remember, this script is just a starting point. Feel free to personalize it based on your specific products, industry, and target audience. Adapt it to your style and the unique needs of the doctor's office you're contacting.

The ultimate aim is to become so familiar and comfortable with the script and anticipated objections that you can effortlessly deliver it. Practice is key—you should rehearse on your own, in front of a mirror, with colleagues, friends, and family. However, the most impactful training, albeit nerve-wracking, is on-the-job experience. When you feel confident enough, try implementing the script with actual leads. This will not only help you refine the script but also enhance your comfort and confidence levels. If you're already in sales but not utilizing scripts, take action as we discussed in Chapter 1. Start creating your scripts now and use them to effectively address objections and increase your closing rate.

Chapter 8: Closing techniques

"You just can't beat the person who never gives up" - Babe Ruth

In this chapter, we will extensively explore the art of closing the sale. From my experience, there are five highly effective closing strategies that you should master. Understanding when and how to utilize each strategy is crucial for achieving the desired results. These strategies are as follows:

1. The Assumptive Close

2. The Direct Close

3. The Option Close

4. The Suggestion Close

5. The Urgency Close

While there may be numerous closing techniques suggested on various websites, as someone who has been selling for nearly 25 years since the age of 11, I can confidently say that these five techniques are the go-to options. By focusing on mastering these strategies, you will have five powerful tools at your disposal when it comes to closing deals. Remember, your relationship and rapport with the client will help you determine the most suitable approach. If the initial close doesn't work, reevaluate the previous steps of the sales process to identify the specific objection and try again.

1. The Assumptive Close

The assumptive close is a closing technique that involves assuming the sale and proceeding as if the prospect has already made the decision to purchase. It is based on the principle that people tend to follow the lead of others and conform to social norms. By assuming the sale, you create an atmosphere of confidence and expectation, subtly influencing the prospect to align their decision with your assumption.

It's actually quite straightforward. With the assumptive close, we operate under the assumption that the client is prepared to proceed. As sales professionals, we have fulfilled our responsibilities. Rather than explicitly asking for the sale, we smoothly transition into the next steps. For instance, you might say, "All that remains is some paperwork. Let's head over to my computer," or "I just need a copy of your ID to initiate the process." By assuming the sale, we convey our control over the process. However, it's essential to have already established the know, like, and trust factors through relationship-building and a strong rapport with the customer.

If you haven't established the know, like, and trust factor in your relationship, it's important to consider alternative approaches that may be more suitable and confident.

Alternatively, you can focus on continuing to build the relationship and strengthen the bond before attempting the assumptive close. If you attempt it too early and encounter resistance, it doesn't necessarily mean you'll lose the deal. It simply indicates that you may have chosen the wrong closing technique or made the attempt prematurely. As you gain more experience, you'll become better at recognizing signs that your client is ready to progress. Remember, it's through trial and error, along with persistence, that you'll improve and develop the ability to identify those opportune moments.

While it's important to note that everyone is different and signs can vary from person to person, there are some general physical cues that may indicate someone is ready to make a purchase. Here are a few potential signs to look out for:

-Body language: Positive body language such as leaning in, maintaining eye contact, nodding, or mirroring your gestures can indicate interest and engagement. It suggests that the person is actively listening and considering what you're saying.

-Facial expressions: Look for signs of enthusiasm, excitement, or a genuine smile. These expressions suggest that the person might be emotionally invested in the product or service and is receptive to making a purchase.

-Asking specific questions: When someone starts asking more detailed questions about the product or service, pricing, warranties, or delivery options, it indicates an increased level of interest and intention to make a purchase.

-Expressing commitment: If the person begins discussing logistics, such as installation, scheduling, or financing options, it shows a willingness to move forward and take the necessary steps to complete the transaction.

Utilizing these indicators to select the most suitable closing technique will determine whether you secure the sale immediately or add the prospect to your CRM for future follow-up. Recognizing and responding to these signs can significantly impact your sales outcomes.

2. The direct close (Ask for the sale):

The direct close is the simplest and most straightforward of all closing techniques. It involves directly asking for the sale without the need for excessive confidence or extraordinary sales skills. For instance, using phrases like "Are you ready to proceed with the paperwork?" or "It seems like you're ready to move forward. Shall we proceed to the next step?" The direct close may be basic, but it's highly effective because if you don't ask, you won't receive. This is a recommended closing technique for most individuals, and even seasoned sales professionals find it valuable. In situations where I sensed my potential clients desired a less pressurized environment based on their body language, I often opted for a gentle approach by asking for the sale. For example, I might say, "Do you have any more questions, or should I start preparing the paperwork?" or something simple like "How does that sound to you?" This approach provides them with a gentle push to make a decision while maintaining a comfortable atmosphere.

There are several body language cues that might indicate someone is not ready to do the deal. Here are a few examples:

1. Closed or crossed arms: This gesture can indicate defensiveness or resistance. It suggests that the person may be hesitant or guarded about moving forward with the purchase.

2. Avoiding eye contact: When someone avoids making eye contact, it can signal discomfort or lack of confidence. They may not feel fully convinced or ready to commit to the purchase.

3. Leaning away or backward: Physical distancing, such as leaning away from you or leaning backward, can suggest a subconscious desire to create space or maintain a sense of personal boundaries. It may indicate that the person is not fully engaged or receptive to the sales pitch.

4. Fidgeting or restless movements: Continuous fidgeting, such as tapping fingers, bouncing legs, or shifting weight, can indicate nervousness or inner turmoil. It may imply that the person is uncertain or hesitant about making a buying decision.

5. Lack of enthusiasm or facial expressions: If the person appears unresponsive, lacks enthusiasm, or displays a neutral facial expression, it could suggest a lack of interest or readiness to make a purchase. They may not be emotionally invested in the product or service.

It is crucial to be attentive to the signals your potential clients are giving you, as your ability to interpret these signals can significantly impact your closing ratio. As mentioned earlier, if you struggle with reading people effectively, considering a class on the DISC assessment could be beneficial. Additionally, conducting research on how to read people through online platforms like YouTube can provide you with valuable information. Embrace a mindset of continuous learning and improvement, always seeking out new knowledge to expand your skills and expertise.

For those new to sales, the direct close is an ideal starting point. However, even experienced salespeople can utilize this technique selectively. By carefully observing and understanding the client's preferences, you can identify when a more subtle and non-aggressive approach is necessary. The direct close serves as a gentle invitation to guide the client towards the closing stage, catering to their desire for a less pushy sales experience.

3. The option close

The option close, also known as the "this or that" close, is a straightforward and effective closing technique. It can be applied in various industries and everyday situations. For instance, in the wireless industry, I frequently used this technique when customers were deciding between two phones they liked. I would simplify the choice by saying, "So, do you prefer the Galaxy S or the Google Pixel?"

If the customer seemed indecisive, I would assist them in making a decision by offering insights such as, "If I were in your shoes, I would go with the Galaxy S if you prioritize a larger screen, or the Pixel if you value better battery life." This guidance helped customers identify the feature that mattered most to them and facilitated their decision-making process.

Although I primarily use business-related examples, the option close can be applied in personal situations as well. Consider that familiar scenario when you and someone else can't decide where to have dinner. You can employ this approach by saying, "Well, I'm torn between Chipotle and Five Guys. Which one do you prefer?" This technique helps individuals in various contexts make choices by presenting clear options.

It's worth noting that sales techniques and principles are not limited to business interactions. Sales strategies are omnipresent in our lives, whether it's the persuasive messages delivered through our phones or the influence of loved ones suggesting weekend plans. Once you adopt a sales mindset, you'll discover how it can enhance your life in numerous ways.

Another valuable social media tip for generating engagement is to use "this or that" polls. I have found that these types of posts tend to receive the highest level of interaction. It's as simple as sharing two pictures or options and asking your audience to vote, such as Starbucks vs. Dunkin Donuts. The response and engagement I receive from these polls are remarkable.

If you find yourself struggling to decide on a paint color for a house flipping project, you can leverage social media by posting two options with a poll and letting the public have a say. Not only does this approach help you make decisions, but it also adds an interactive element that keeps your followers engaged.

By consistently posting interesting and compelling content, you'll not only attract more followers but also maintain their interest and participation. Social media platforms provide a great opportunity to connect with your audience and build a strong online presence.

4.   The Suggestion close

The essence of this technique is clear: There will inevitably be clients who struggle to make a decision without your guidance. This situation is quite common in real estate, where you might show clients numerous properties, gaining an understanding of their preferences along the way. However, even when presenting them with the perfect home that meets all their criteria, something seems to be holding them back.

This is when you must step in and explicitly communicate that this is indeed the right choice for them. Addressing them directly, you might say, "John & Sara, after considering countless options, this home not only fulfills all your requirements but also surpasses them. I believe we should move forward with this one." It's crucial to be direct and concise, as you have gathered all the necessary information and found the ideal home. It's time to make a decision.

If, at this point, they still hesitate, it's important to inquire about their concerns. Their reasoning should be compelling, as any other explanation may indicate it's time to cut ties and focus on other clients. I also applied this approach in the wireless industry. For instance, if a customer keeps showing interest in a particular phone after several interactions, you can gently nudge them by saying, "I've noticed you've been eyeing that phone and seem quite excited about it. If I were in your shoes, I would go for it—it's an excellent device that won't disappoint. And remember, there's always a return policy if you change your mind." Sometimes, reassuring them that the decision isn't set in stone can push them closer to taking the plunge.

Confidence is key when employing this closing technique, particularly with individuals who struggle with indecisiveness. With the right approach, it can be highly effective in helping them overcome their hesitations and move forward with a choice.

5. The urgency close

All successful businesses employ the urgency close in their marketing strategies to compel people to take immediate action. This approach creates a sense of urgency, prompting individuals to make quick decisions out of fear of missing out (FOMO). Numerous techniques can be utilized, such as emphasizing limited stock with statements like "I only have one left in stock" or highlighting impending price increases with phrases like "Tomorrow, the price goes up." These tactics effectively prompt customers to act decisively.

Prominent retailers utilize doorbusters, restaurants entice customers during slow periods with happy hours or kids eat free deals, and Amazon employs temporary price reductions on wish-listed products to induce purchases. Amazon's ingenious approach includes providing shoppers with a tool to create and share wish lists, leading to personalized deals tailored to individual preferences. This strategy not only appears helpful to customers but also serves Amazon's purpose of increasing sales. Additionally, Amazon can monetize this information by selling it to interested third parties seeking potential customers.

In the automotive industry, time-limited financing deals and sign-and-drive offers are common urgency closes. However, there is a particular urgency close employed in the auto industry that I strongly dislike. It involves a dealer presenting a piece of paper and pressuring you to sign immediately in order to secure a specific price. This approach is unethical and contributes to the negative perception of car salespeople as deceitful and untrustworthy. Personally, I would never engage in such tactics.

If you observe carefully, you'll notice various instances of urgency closes in your daily life. It is perhaps the most widely used sales technique, often masquerading as advertising while effectively closing sales. The lure of limited-time offers or one-day sales can trigger the thought of "I wanted that item, and it's on sale only today?!" In real estate, the highest and best offer approach serves as an exceptional urgency close. When multiple offers are on the table, sellers encourage potential buyers to submit their best offer promptly, Isn't it great to witness someone's ultimate offer?

Incorporating the urgency close into your sales pitch is crucial. There are ample opportunities to employ this technique, and it boasts a high success rate, particularly with impulse buyers. According to social.com, 95% of Americans make impulse purchases, highlighting the need to leverage this aspect of human behavior to your advantage.

To summarize, these five options are what I consider to be the top choices for most sales professionals. While there are countless techniques out there, these have proven to be effective in closing deals both in professional and personal settings. Even in the realm of dating, sales skills come into play. Take, for instance, a clever pickup line by renowned rapper Lil Dicky: "Excuse me, what's your availability as far as being hit on right now? Like are you open-minded to that type of thing or not even remotely?" This line stands out because it is unique, non-aggressive, and demonstrates genuine concern for the other person's feelings. Embracing new selling approaches is always beneficial. Once I achieved satisfactory sales numbers, I constantly explored new tactics. It was a low-risk endeavor as it wouldn't harm my existing results, but if successful, it meant adding a fantastic new pitch to my repertoire.

Chapter 9: Power of positive thinking

"In order to carry a positive action we must develop a positive vision" - Dalai Lama

I must emphasize the importance of mindset in achieving successful outcomes. One key aspect that always comes to mind is the power of positive thinking. Maintaining a positive outlook even in the face of adversity can inspire others to follow you, instill confidence in your customers, and attract people to your presence. Mastering this skill is challenging but incredibly crucial.

Reflect on some of the worst experiences you've had in life and consider how you handled them. I learned this valuable lesson at a young age from my mother. Despite the hardships she faced, she always saw the glass as half full. Whenever something negative occurred, she would tell me, "Kiddo, everything happens for a reason. I believe that if you learn from this experience, you'll emerge stronger." It was remarkable to witness her positive mindset, even in the midst of difficult circumstances. I'm certain it wasn't easy for her, but she made it happen.

When I experienced heartbreak, my mother found ways to extract positivity from the situation or at least uncover a silver lining. When our trailer burned down, leaving us with nothing, she looked at me and said, "We lost material possessions, but you know what we didn't lose? Each other."

I have applied this approach to every challenging situation in my life. Sometimes, I need to step away momentarily and gather my thoughts, but I firmly believe there's a positive aspect to every situation if you truly contemplate it.

Lost a valuable client? Ask yourself what you could have done differently and use it as a learning experience to avoid losing more valuable clients in the future.

Going through a breakup? Recall all the positive experiences you shared with that person and learn from the negatives, striving to improve your future self and future relationships.

Experiencing car troubles? View it as an opportunity to delve into the automotive industry, perhaps considering leasing your next vehicle so that any future breakdowns become someone else's concern.

I once had a vehicle break down on my way to an appointment that had the potential to generate over $10,000 in revenue. As a result, I chose to lease my next vehicle for $255 per month over 36 months. If I had started leasing earlier, the revenue from that missed appointment would have covered my entire lease, with an additional $900 to spare. This is precisely why I now opt for leasing, as automobiles are not built the way they used to be. I'm almost certain that cars are designed to last approximately 60-72 months, the typical financing term for a purchase. If, like me, you have minimal knowledge of car repairs, it's essential to either acquire the necessary skills or place yourself in a better situation where you don't have to worry about fixing them.

Any negativity lingering in your mind is merely a distraction from your ultimate goal. Embracing a negative mindset will undoubtedly hinder your potential for success. For me, the power of positive thinking acts as a tool to combat negativity. Instead of fixating on the negative aspects, I ask myself, "What lesson can I learn from this?" or "How can I improve this situation despite its challenges?" More often than not, I find a way to transform negativity into something positive.

Take, for instance, the devastating incident of my childhood home burning down. If that had never occurred, my life would undoubtedly have taken a completely different path. A few months after the fire, my mother made the decision to relocate to Buckeye, the largest suburb of Phoenix, Arizona. It was in Buckeye that I crossed paths with the woman I eventually married. Although our marriage has since ended, she remains an important figure in my life. She is an exceptional mother, and I hold great love, care, and admiration for her. This brings me to my main point: had my home not burned down, I would never have met her or had the incredible blessing of raising our two amazing children. Thus, one of the most challenging events in my life ultimately led to two of the most significant joys I have ever experienced.

So, when you reflect on the traumatic events that have occurred in your own life, consider the bigger picture. What lessons did you learn? What changes did you make? What future outcomes unfolded as a result?

I recall the day I was fired from my position at T-Mobile USA, despite my eight-plus years of service, multiple awards, and ranking in the top 2% of sales nationwide. The termination was due to an unauthorized $25 discount. I was devastated. My wife was pregnant with our second child, and I lost not only my income but also my benefits, unvested stock options, and over two hundred hours of accumulated paid time off. The total loss exceeded six figures, and I had no idea what my next move would be. To make matters worse, this occurred just three days before Christmas.

However, let's shift our focus to the positive outcomes that emerged from this situation. First and foremost, I had the opportunity to spend the holidays—Christmas and New Year's—with my wife and daughter, free from the demands of a retail job. My wife, my rock, encouraged me to take a risk on myself. Although I held a real estate license, I had never truly dedicated the time to develop that aspect of my career. She believed in me, supported me, and trusted that I could make it happen. Without her unwavering support, I might have resorted to seeking employment with another wireless company in the nearby mall. Instead, on January 1st, I redirected my focus toward building my real estate business. That six-figure loss, the stress of being uninsured with a family to support, and the anxiety of losing my primary source of income all served as fuel for my determination. I can confidently say that I would not be where I am today if I hadn't been fired. My previous position offered comfort, generous compensation, and exceptional benefits. Yet, those traumatic events—losing my home and my job—shaped my character and compelled me toward success.

Moreover, I continually set and achieve new goals, constantly raising the bar for myself. I am genuinely grateful for being fired and for the loss of my childhood home. These two profoundly challenging events molded me into the person I am today and propelled me toward success.

The power of positive thinking should extend beyond significant life events; it should permeate every aspect of our lives—every day, every hour, every minute. Allowing negativity to creep in at any moment only serves as a distraction from the abundance of positivity that surrounds us. Let it be known that these words are not mere ink on paper; they hold the key to unlocking doors you never imagined would swing open. If there's one takeaway from this book, it is that embracing positive thinking has the power to utterly transform your life.

Chapter 10: Relentless follow up

"Not following up with your prospects is the same as filling up your bathtub without first putting the stopper in the drain" - Michelle Moore

Just yesterday, I had a meeting with one of my agents who is facing challenges when it comes to converting the leads I provide. Yes, I do supply leads to my agents, while I teach them how to generate leads themselves. As they continue to depend on the leads I provide, my profitability increases due to the fact that our company's leads are compensated at a lower split. My agent asked me a straightforward question: "When is a lead considered dead?" I gave him a simple answer: "When they explicitly tell you to stop contacting them in an impolite manner." Otherwise, that lead is signaling that I need to exert more effort and explore alternative ways of communication.

Earlier in this book, I discussed the importance of using a CRM as a second brain, and a crucial aspect of that is maintaining detailed notes on the last contact attempt and the communication method used. If the last interaction was a text message with no response, try reaching out through a phone call or email. If multiple attempts have been made with no success, consider searching for additional contact information such as alternate phone numbers or social media accounts. If all else fails, look up their address and send a personalized letter along with your business card. And if that still doesn't yield results, if you happen to be in their vicinity, pay them a visit and present a small gift—it's difficult to harbor ill feelings towards someone who offers a thoughtful gesture.

A lead represents your future income, and neglecting to explore all avenues to convert that lead brings you closer to financial struggle. Each lead should be treated as a vital asset to your business, and if they are unresponsive, there must be a reason. It's crucial to exhaust all available options. Our background software allows us to locate individuals, verify contact information, and even find their current residence for mailing or door-knocking purposes. We also leverage this software to identify their household members, providing an opportunity to engage with an alternate contact if necessary. You must be willing to try every conceivable approach and treat every lead as if it were your sole lead. Even when you deem a lead as inactive, I recommend periodically reaching out, perhaps once a quarter, unless they have explicitly requested not to be contacted.

In the sales realm, you will often hear the term "nurture," which involves caring for and fostering the growth of someone or something. Even a simple step like enrolling them in an automated email campaign is better than doing nothing. While I'm not a major proponent of solely relying on automated emails, it still surpasses complete inactivity. I previously discussed the concept of the "33 touch rule," where a monthly email constitutes 12 of the 33 touches. But what else can you do? Utilize their mailing address to send holiday cards, monthly market newsletters, or postcards featuring valuable content such as great cooking recipes. By devising a game plan and putting it into action, creating a 33 touch strategy for everyone in your database, including your inactive leads, becomes a manageable task.

Many of us underestimate the power of social media, which is an invaluable tool that is freely available to everyone. According to statista.com, approximately 82% of Americans actively use social media platforms. If you're unable to reach someone through traditional means, try locating their social media profiles. Send them a follow request and kindly explain that you may have outdated contact information and would like to update your records.

In the real estate industry, renters often begin their search for a new place towards the end of their lease. However, by that time, it's usually too late to secure a new property. As a result, they may ignore or "ghost" the agents they were previously in contact with because they decide to renew their lease for another 12 months. By identifying this pattern, you can proactively set expectations with renters, advising them to get pre-approved and start looking about halfway through their lease. Furthermore, you can schedule a follow-up reminder to call them in four months, reminding them that it's time to initiate the process. Additionally, offering to review their lease can be a helpful strategy.

Sometimes, terminating a lease may not incur substantial penalties, providing an opportunity to pitch them on starting their property search immediately.

In addition, remember to provide valuable information to tenants regarding the advantages of buying versus renting. Many tenants are unaware that their rental payments cover the landlord's mortgage and generate profit for them. Furthermore, most individuals lack a comprehensive understanding of how equity functions, despite it being one of the most influential financial instruments available. It is our duty to educate our clients on the value of what we offer. By providing them with ample information to make informed decisions, you increase the likelihood of securing their business and closing deals more efficiently compared to a less proactive approach with follow-ups.

It is essential to think outside the box and employ various approaches when dealing with unresponsive leads. Remember, their lack of response does not necessarily equate to a definitive "no". Many agents have dismissed internet leads as ineffective, but perhaps they didn't invest sufficient effort into working them diligently. While it's true that people may provide inaccurate information, it becomes your responsibility to delve deeper, adopting an investigative mindset to uncover the correct details.

I have extensively discussed the importance of client relationship management software (CRM), but ultimately, the specific tool you use is not as crucial as having a system in place to store all the necessary contact information and notes.

Whether it is a CRM software, a spreadsheet, or a simple notebook, what matters most is how effectively you utilize it. While CRMs offer convenient reminder functions, you can achieve similar results using a calendar or notepad. If the cost is a barrier to adopting a CRM, consider Hubspot's free basic CRM, which provides a solid starting point, albeit with some feature limitations. To ensure adequate client record-keeping, here is a list of essential information to maintain for each client:

1. Full Name
2. Email
3. Cell Phone
4. Address

It's important to highlight that if any of the mentioned information is missing, you should make an effort to obtain it. If your clients are still in communication, kindly ask them for the required details. Otherwise, you may need to adopt a detective mindset and employ tools to locate the missing information. If you find yourself in the situation where you are working with a limited budget, there are free online resources available, such as truepeoplesearch.com, that can assist you in finding the necessary information.

Above, you'll find the essential information, but I prefer to maintain comprehensive client profiles that include the following details:

- Birthday (of both clients if married)
- Place of work

- Social media accounts
- Home buying anniversary (For real estate)
- Kids names, ages, hobbies
- Pets names and breeds
- Favorite food
- Favorite adult beverages
- Hobbies
- Favorite sports teams
- Date of last contact
- Last form of contact
- Preferred contact method
- History of business done together
- Business referrals I have given them

Having as much information as possible is always beneficial. It's likely that the database you're using may not have specific fields for all the details mentioned earlier. In such cases, the "notes" section becomes crucial as it allows you to store additional information. This can be particularly useful when you receive referrals and want to show gratitude by giving them a personalized gift based on their preferences.

The majority of CRM systems available in the market offer a hashtag system that enables you to categorize your clients using tags. It is crucial to utilize this feature effectively. As your database grows, having the ability to send bulk emails to specific groups such as past clients or clients of a particular type becomes much simpler when you have tags to sort and organize them. This feature proves to be highly valuable in managing a large database efficiently.

Here's an instance demonstrating how you can leverage your CRM to generate business. Suppose you have set up a hashtag for past clients as #pastclient in your CRM. You can send a mass email to your #pastclient database, informing them about your referral program where they can earn prizes for each client they refer to you. You can send out these emails periodically, and the prizes can be as simple as small gift cards. It's remarkable how much more motivated people become to seek referrals when incentivized and rewarded for their efforts.

I once had the pleasure of working with an exceptional lender who had a remarkable follow-up approach. Every Monday morning, he would call to engage in friendly conversations about weekend events, sports, family, and more. During our discussions, he would provide updates on our ongoing business transactions and offer to schedule our next lunch appointment. However, what truly stood out was his thoughtfulness. Knowing that I was a Dallas Cowboys fan, despite living in Pittsburgh, Pennsylvania, he went the extra mile. Each year, he created sports calendars for his clients and agents, and he ordered the minimum quantity (250) for the Cowboys. Remarkably, I was the only Cowboys fan among his clients. This display of out-of-the-box thinking and making me feel special truly inspired me to provide him with more business. I estimate that the magnetic calendar he got for me must have cost him over $500. As a humorous gesture one year, he even gifted me all 250 calendars he had ordered.

During my time at T-Mobile USA, we didn't have access to a CRM system. However, we made use of a system called a

B-Back binder, which proved to be effective despite its outdated nature. The binder had sections for each day of the month and the months of the year, allowing us to schedule follow-ups accordingly. Even though it wasn't technologically advanced, it worked as long as we remained committed to following up with our leads as promised. If you prefer non-technological solutions, you can find alternative methods that suit your needs.

Personally, I used an Excel spreadsheet for many years to manage my client information. The key is to find a system that works for you and, most importantly, to consistently utilize it.

A sales professional who excels in relentless follow-up will experience significantly more success than one who relies solely on inbound business. While building strong relationships can lead to clients reaching out to you based on their positive impressions, actively working your existing book of business will undoubtedly result in higher conversion rates. It's surprising how many sales professionals invest significant amounts, even thousands or tens of thousands of dollars, each month in acquiring new leads, yet neglect the potential of their old or inactive leads and fail to effectively engage with past clients and their sphere of influence.

Chapter 11: Networking

"Networking is an investment in your business. It takes time and when done correctly can yield great results for years to come" -Diane Helbig

When I ventured into the real estate industry, I quickly recognized the paramount importance of networking in establishing my business. As I was not originally from Pittsburgh, my acquaintances were limited to my colleagues at T-Mobile and the individuals my wife interacted with at Walmart. Networking became the cornerstone of expanding my local sphere of influence. Irrespective of the sales field you find yourself in, networking has the potential to greatly enhance your business. While at T-Mobile, I primarily relied on the influx of customers to generate business, but I realized that I could have expanded my client base further had I possessed the knowledge and skills to network effectively outside the store. In the following sections, I will delve into various forms of networking, most of which are applicable regardless of the sales domain you operate in.

The initial form of networking I refer to as "one on one" involves meeting individuals with the intention of establishing a connection. This could include friends or family members. Spending quality time with someone and getting to know them brings you closer to developing a KLT relationship—knowing, liking, and trusting one another. If there's someone you haven't had a conversation with in a while, take the initiative to call them and suggest meeting up for coffee or a drink. Express your desire to reconnect and explore how you can mutually benefit each other's lives and businesses. We commonly refer to this group as our sphere of influence, and it is essential to add these individuals to your database as well.

Another form of networking is known as category-specific networking. There are numerous groups available, but one notable example is BNI (Business Networking International), which is likely the largest global network. BNI organizes weekly meetings where participants gather to educate each other about their respective businesses and exchange qualified referrals. This type of group proves to be highly beneficial for various sales endeavors.

I vividly recall the experience of a friend who joined my BNI group. He had recently started an electrician side job and aimed to transition to full-time business ownership within five years. Surprisingly, within just a month of joining BNI, he received such a substantial influx of business that he decided to quit his primary job. The increased business from BNI allowed him to cover his expenses solely through his new business venture.

If I had known about BNI during my time in the wireless industry, I would have undoubtedly joined a large chapter meeting at 7 am, even before my store opened. Each time I sold a cell phone, I typically earned $30 to $100 in commission. Joining BNI costs approximately $600 per year, and a sizable chapter in my area boasts 40 to 50 members.

Assuming a conservative estimate of selling a plan to 70% of the group, even at the lowest commission rate of $30, I would have earned $1200, yielding a considerable return on my $600 investment. Moreover, this calculation doesn't take into account the potential for additional referrals. Undoubtedly, this form of networking possesses significant potential and holds great power for business growth.

The final major type of networking is known as large group networking, exemplified by events organized by chambers of commerce and similar organizations. Attending these gatherings provides ample opportunities to network with numerous individuals, including those within your industry. To make the most of these events, it is essential to actively engage and move around the room. Introduce yourself to people, exchange business cards, and establish connections. For individuals who may not immediately catch your interest as potential networking partners, you can add them to your database using a designated hashtag like #networking. This way, your system can automatically send them follow-up emails.

As for individuals whom you genuinely connected with and wish to develop a deeper relationship, reach out to them the following day. Express your delight in meeting them and extend an invitation for a coffee or lunch meeting to further acquaint yourselves with one another. Emphasize your desire to establish a mutually beneficial referral relationship if they are interested. This proactive approach can foster fruitful connections and expand your network.

There are numerous ways to engage in networking, both online and offline. Personally, I prefer face-to-face interactions, as meeting people in person allows for deeper connections. The more individuals you meet and establish relationships with, the more beneficial it will be for your business. You can even consider initiating your own networking group focused on educating people about your trade or product. For instance, at our office, we conduct seminars on real estate investment strategies with minimal upfront costs. These seminars are attended by over fifty people, and we charge a fee of $100 per attendee. Hosting such events can not only provide revenue but also position you as an authority in your field, attracting individuals who are eager to learn about the topic. Platforms like meetup.com, facebook.com, and eventbrite.com can assist you in organizing and promoting your events. Although the initial turnout may be small, hosting regular events will gradually attract larger audiences.

Let me provide you with an example: One of our agents started hosting a monthly real estate investor meeting at a local brewery, offering it for free as long as attendees ordered food and drinks. Initially, only a few people attended, but over time, the attendance grew to over fifty individuals. This demonstrates the power of consistent networking efforts. Even if you invite guest speakers to add value to the events, people will perceive you as an expert and seek to build relationships with you, ultimately becoming potential clients or partners. Networking doesn't necessarily have to revolve around business topics alone. Personally, I belong to a group of individuals who gather to play basketball a few times a week at 5:30 am. By regularly participating in these basketball sessions, I have built strong relationships with the group members and have acquired agents and clients over the years without actively pursuing them.

To fully capitalize on your sales potential, it is crucial to actively engage in personal interactions and connect with others. Relying solely on inbound business may yield some results for certain individuals, but it is unlikely to lead to genuine success in most cases.

Chapter 12: Business to business relationships

"The only way to consistently grow in B2B is to be better than very good" - Seth Godin

Fostering business-to-business relationships is a crucial aspect that I should have prioritized earlier in my life. However, without awareness of its potential impact and how it can benefit you, it is easy to overlook. Although this chapter will not be lengthy, its significance should not be underestimated. Building upon the previous chapter on networking, exploring the realm of business-to-business interactions can enhance your referral business and establish a network of professionals whom you can refer to and seek advice from.

The B2B sector offers some of the most valuable referral relationships, as business owners understand the importance of fostering such connections for growth. In the real estate industry, it is crucial to network with lenders, mortgage brokers, title companies, attorneys, and CPAs, as they can facilitate mutually beneficial relationships. These professionals directly interact with clients who may require your services, just as you can refer clients to them.

While any business can potentially serve as a referral source, it is wise to prioritize those that directly collaborate with or complement your industry. For instance, an automotive sales professional should establish relationships with mechanics, insurance brokers, and lenders. Business referral relationships have the potential to generate a higher volume of referrals compared to individual consumers. Therefore, it is essential to establish clear communication regarding the goals and expectations of the relationship. Although these conversations may feel slightly awkward, they are paramount in setting the foundation for building our businesses, while also maintaining a friendly rapport.

The conversation could go something like this: "Brad, I appreciate you taking the time to meet with me. It's evident that our industries have synergies, and I believe we could establish a strong referral relationship. My aim in getting to know you better is to mutually connect each other with potential clients. Are you open to building this type of partnership?"

In cases where they may not have many leads to offer but you have ample opportunities for them, it's crucial to explore alternative ways they can support your business. For instance, they might consider contributing to a joint farming campaign or allocating funds to your marketing budget. However, if they are unable to provide any assistance, it's important to identify this upfront. This allows you to make informed decisions and swiftly redirect your efforts towards building relationships with other professionals in their industry.

Had I possessed the knowledge I have now, I undoubtedly would have experienced greater success during my early years as an agent. Take, for example, my relationship with the lender I mentioned earlier in this book. He was exceptional, excelling in follow-up, beloved by my clients, and treated me like family. However, if I had understood how to leverage that relationship, I could have gained even more. Specifically, if I had communicated to him the significant number of referrals I was providing him compared to the referrals he was giving me, I could have persuaded him to contribute to additional marketing efforts that would have driven more business for both of us.

During the five-plus years we worked together, he may have only provided me with five referrals, whereas I consistently directed all my business to him, averaging three to five quality leads per month or more. Unbeknownst to me, I held significant leverage in our relationship. He would have done everything possible to ensure I continued to send him business, rather than seeking out another lender. But I never realized that I could ask for more.

In our industry, even a modest amount, let's say $250 per month, could have generated an additional 5-25 leads for me. Considering my high conversion rate, let's assume I converted 7 leads per month from his marketing dollars. This would have amounted to an extra three hundred thousand dollars in annual revenue based on my average sales price at that time. Moreover, it would have provided him with a favorable return on investment, likely prompting him to increase his marketing budget over time.

A savvy agent maintains multiple relationships with lenders, allowing different lenders to cover different lead sources (e.g., Tod pays for Zillow, Jim pays for Realtor.com), thereby driving even more business. While I cannot change the past, what I can do is share my knowledge to teach others how to leverage these business-to-business relationships. In the next chapter, I will provide a comprehensive breakdown of the value my team of B2B partners brings to my business. This is meant to stimulate your thinking about the composition of your own team.

Although I have primarily used examples from the wireless and real estate industries throughout this book, these strategies can be applied to any sales business. The key is to identify business professionals who have access to the same client base as you and find ways to mutually support each other's growth. For instance, if I were a software sales professional specializing in CRM systems, I would seek relationships with sales professionals offering complementary software solutions. Additionally, I would focus on individuals involved in servicing the industries I target, as they can provide warm introductions to potential clients. While I emphasize my specific industries of experience, this approach is applicable across various sectors.

If you haven't prioritized B2B relationships, this is an important insight for you. Even if you already have such relationships, I would venture to say that you are not fully leveraging their potential. It is crucial to engage in those initially uncomfortable yet highly rewarding conversations that clearly articulate your expectations. A successful relationship between us depends on both parties adding substantial value to each other's businesses.

Chapter 13: Team of professionals

"If everyone is moving forward together, then success takes care of itself" - Henry Ford

We are now embarking on a comprehensive exploration of the professionals comprising my team and their instrumental role in shaping my current success. While it may be possible to pursue a sales career in isolation, why would you choose to do so? It is wiser to work smart rather than work hard alone. These individuals are motivated to generate business for you because you reciprocate by sending business their way, not only from your personal endeavors but also through referrals of your clients, friends, family, and more. Below, I present actual examples of the members on my team:

Mentor-

I begin with mentioning my mentor. Although your mentor may not directly contribute to your business referrals, they are an integral part of your team and will have the most significant impact. Currently, my mentor also serves as my partner, consistently offering support and bringing a unique perspective that differs from my own. With extensive experience, my mentor has been instrumental in shaping my career. In return, I bring value to his professional journey by infusing energy, motivation, and a technologically-driven mindset into our company. Without each other, our individual paths would have taken different trajectories.

My mentor has imparted invaluable knowledge about the industry and has shown genuine concern for my personal growth and investment endeavors. He has taught me how to leverage resources such as other people's money to foster growth, the art of selling real estate, and the importance of maximizing productivity. One particular lesson that I often share is the concept of assigning a value to one's time. For instance, let us say that value is $100 per hour. When my mentor initially introduced this idea, that was approximately the value I placed on my time. While my valuation may have increased since then, the mindset remains the same. By adopting this perspective, any task that costs less than $100 per hour should be delegated to others. This approach is truly ingenious.

In fact, when I brought someone on board to handle task-based work within my business, a significant burden was lifted off my shoulders. The money invested in that individual's support translates into far greater financial returns as I can now focus on revenue-generating activities. Let me give you an example. If it takes you two hours to clean your house and you can hire someone for less than $100 per hour, it makes sense to delegate the task. However, it is crucial to utilize the newfound free time to pursue money-making opportunities rather than succumbing to laziness.

These small yet wise teachings have greatly improved my life. If you don't already have a mentor, prioritizing finding one should be your number one goal for both personal and business development.

Attorney-

Attorneys are invaluable assets to any business, and they also have a wealth of business referrals to offer. Personally, I have established trust and strong connections with two attorneys, one of whom is Matt. Over time, Matt has not only become a trusted friend but also a reliable source of free legal advice. In return, he often seeks my expertise in my trade, creating a mutually beneficial relationship.

What sets Matt apart is his extensive education and diverse background. Prior to becoming an attorney, he worked as an engineer and also practiced family law before specializing in business law. This breadth of experience allows him to provide valuable insights and guidance across various areas. Since collaborating with Matt, he has connected me with an impressive number of potential clients, which I estimate to be over fifty. While I cannot provide an exact count, it is evident that his contributions have been significant.

The beauty of working with attorneys lies in their specific areas of expertise. By networking and fostering relationships with attorneys specializing in divorce, family law, business, real estate, estate planning, elder law, criminal law, labor law, health law, tax law, intellectual property, corporate law, insurance law, environmental law, and more, you can tap into a diverse network of professionals. I recommend selecting the top two or three attorneys whose expertise aligns with your business needs and initiating the process of building fruitful relationships that will benefit both parties involved.

CPA-

My initial CPA (Certified Public Accountant) was by far one of the biggest assholes I know. Despite claiming to welcome any questions, he would often respond with condescension and belittle me for asking. However, despite his poor interpersonal skills, he did impart valuable knowledge about minimizing tax obligations. Through his guidance, I have come remarkably close to paying minimal or no taxes while experiencing increased financial success. Eventually, his services became too costly, prompting me to switch to a new CPA more recently.

Despite the unpleasant interactions, it is important to acknowledge that my original CPA and I maintained a fruitful referral relationship. Over the years, he referred numerous clients to me, and in return, I reciprocated. Furthermore, he connected me with private individuals willing to lend money for the acquisition of distressed real estate properties. The significance of a good CPA cannot be overstated—they are essential for managing personal finances effectively. However, a great CPA goes beyond that, actively contributing to business growth. Establishing a strong relationship with a highly competent CPA should be a top priority in your business endeavors.

Over the next five years, one of my objectives is to establish an in-house accountant dedicated to managing all aspects of our business finances. This strategic move aims to streamline and enhance our financial operations, ensuring greater accuracy, efficiency, and control.

By having an in-house accountant, we can effectively monitor our financial transactions, maintain up-to-date records, and generate timely financial reports. This level of expertise within our organization will enable us to make informed decisions based on accurate financial data, ultimately contributing to our overall success.

Insurance-

Casey, my insurance broker, played a crucial role in my business. Not only did he excel in providing exceptional service to our clients, but he also went above and beyond to find specialized insurance companies tailored to our specific niches. Casey's expertise allowed us to secure the best possible rates, ensuring our clients received top-notch coverage.

Over the years, Casey also referred some business to me, which, despite insurance agents having fewer referral opportunities compared to other partners, significantly contributed to the growth of my business. Even if it amounted to just a deal or two per year, these referrals made a noticeable impact.

Our relationship took an exciting turn when we decided to open an insurance agency together. While it may take some time for the agency to reach its full potential, the opportunity to establish an additional revenue stream is invaluable. The insurance industry may offer lower initial compensation compared to other sales areas, but its residual model is highly attractive. By retaining clients, we can continue generating income from their policies year after year.

It's important to note that certain aspects of the insurance business offer higher upfront compensation but lack the residual aspect, such as life insurance. If I were starting out as an insurance sales professional, I would focus on a balanced approach, allocating 50% of my efforts to building the home and auto insurance segment of my business, and the remaining 50% to developing my income through life insurance sales. This strategic mix would allow me to establish a strong foundation while maximizing both current income and long-term growth potential.

Lenders-

In my professional field, lenders hold great significance. They play a crucial role on the sales side by either bringing leads to the table or contributing to our marketing efforts. On the investing side, I have formed partnerships with other lenders, particularly in the commercial realm, who facilitate timely refinances for our investment properties.

One lender in particular, Bob, adopts a proactive approach by collaborating with different banks that offer cash-out refinancing. He maximizes his business potential by engaging with these banks until they begin to restrict their lending practices in that particular area. At that point, he seamlessly transitions to another bank. This arrangement benefits me greatly because I can rely on Bob to consistently work with lenders who appreciate my business. It is worth noting that not all lenders facilitate cash-out refinancing for investors. Cash-out refinancing is an immensely valuable tool for real estate investors as it enables us to extract tax-free equity from our properties.

The examples provided thus far highlight the significant influence that can be derived from leveraging these business-to-business relationships. These connections have played a pivotal role in shaping my current position, serving not only as sources of referrals but also as invaluable resources when encountering unfamiliar challenges. It is essential to assemble a team tailored to your specific industry, individuals who can assist you in not only acquiring more business but also addressing any issues specific to their respective fields. Having such a team instills confidence when referring them to your network, thereby contributing to their business growth as well. The value of these relationships extends beyond mere referrals, serving as a support system that fosters mutual success.

Chapter 14: Regrets

"I'd rather regret doing something than not doing something"
-James Hetfield

After much contemplation, I deliberated on whether to include this chapter in the book. However, as I have emphasized throughout the book, every event occurs for a purpose. While I do harbor some regrets, I believe it is crucial to address them openly. In my perspective, we glean more valuable lessons from our failures than from our successes. Without experiencing setbacks, I would not have taken the necessary risks. To achieve greater success, it becomes imperative to select and prioritize where we invest our time and make the required sacrifices.

I draw inspiration from fictional characters like Scrooge McDuck, whom my children often watch in Disney shows and movies. Despite being a fictional character, Scrooge McDuck imparts valuable lessons. What good is amassing enormous wealth if it results in constant grumpiness, unhappiness, and loneliness? While success is invigorating and propels me to strive for excellence, I also ponder the sacrifices I have made to reach my current position.

In the following section, I will candidly list some of my most significant regrets. It is my hope that you can learn from my mistakes and establish healthy boundaries in your own life. By doing so, you can avoid similar regrets and navigate your path towards success with greater wisdom.

-Fatherhood

As a business owner and a father, conflicts in schedules are bound to arise. During the early years of my children's lives, their mother (who was my wife at the time) took on the role of a full-time stay-at-home mother. Looking back, I realize that I may not have been as present as I should have been. I entrusted their mother, who is an exceptional parent, with most of the responsibilities. Although I didn't miss out on a significant number of milestones, there were moments that I wasn't there for, and even when I was home, my focus remained on work.

As my children have grown older and their mother has pursued her own career, the dynamics have shifted, and I find myself cherishing the additional time I spend with them. I am making a conscious effort to prioritize and be more attentive to their needs. If given the chance to go back in time, I would strive to be more focused on being a father. However, I understand that it's easier said than done. Time is limited, and as both a business owner and a father, I cannot afford to neglect either role. It's a constant balancing act that requires my utmost dedication and effort.

-My health

For an entire decade, I neglected my health and allowed myself to reach a weight of over 300 pounds. It was a dangerous path that could have led me towards diabetes and a premature death. In hindsight, I realize that I should have placed more emphasis on my well-being. However, once I shifted my focus and found the motivation to make a change, I was pleasantly surprised by how quickly the weight began to drop off. Adopting a healthier lifestyle became a priority, and although it requires a long-term commitment, I deeply regret not starting earlier in life. We only have one chance at this remarkable journey called life, and it's crucial that we all strive to prolong our time here.

-Career

In retrospect, opening my brokerage was far from the easiest path available to me. Looking back, I realize that I had no idea what I was getting myself into. Although I am extremely pleased with the success and growth of the business, I can not deny that I could have potentially made more money with less effort and time by simply running a team. The insight I had regarding the long-term potential of owning a company was a driving force behind my decision, and I believe it will prove beneficial in the long run. However, as a 30-year-old with a wife and two children, it was a significant undertaking to handle.

Despite my satisfaction with the current state of the business, it does not diminish the fact that I endured countless hours of hard work, dedication, and challenges that I would not have faced if I had chosen the easier option. Perhaps it's a blessing in disguise that I didn't opt for the path of least resistance.

-Finances

While I have successfully built a substantial net worth for someone in their mid-30s, I can't help but contemplate how different things might have looked if I had invested more in stocks and cryptocurrency earlier in life. For instance, in 2015, when I began earning good money, Bitcoin had an average price of $250 per coin. Today, it trades at around $30,000 per coin. If I had invested $1,000 in Bitcoin back then, it would be worth $120,000 now.

Microsoft is a company I have always admired, and I have owned some of their stock for quite some time. In 2015, their stock price was approximately $45 per share, but now it has soared to $336. Even if I had chosen the "safer" route and invested in the S&P 500 in 2015, when it was around $1,900 per share, it would have grown to over $4,000 per share today. The power of long-term investing is undeniably significant, and I was overly focused on real estate, neglecting other opportunities for passive investments.

- Marriage

Recently, I reached the difficult decision to end my marriage with my wife, Kasandra. Over time, we grew apart, and our values no longer aligned as they once did. Despite our

132

differences, I will always hold love and care for her in my heart. Kasandra is an incredible person and an exceptional mother. Reflecting on our journey, I realize that I should have invested more time and effort into our relationship. Perhaps, by prioritizing our connection and nurturing our bond, we could have grown together rather than drifting apart. I acknowledge that it takes both partners to sustain a relationship, and I regret not putting in sufficient effort over the years. This responsibility lies primarily with me.

I firmly believe in the notion that everything happens for a reason. In time, I will discover the purpose behind experiencing this process. It's possible that this phase is meant to grant me a period of solitude, allowing me to discover my true self and work on personal growth. Perhaps, Kasandra and I were not destined to be lifelong partners. While it is unlikely that she will read this book, if by chance she does, I want her to know that I am sincerely sorry for how things unfolded.

I believe it is crucial to include this chapter, despite the personal pain it brings, because it serves as a reminder that success often comes with sacrifices. In retrospect, I realize that I may have sacrificed too much throughout the years, and I do harbor some regrets about that. However, dwelling on the past serves no purpose. Instead, I choose to focus on the present and the future.

On my personal Facebook page, my tagline reads, "Every day I wake up and strive to be better than yesterday." This philosophy encapsulates the essence of our human journey. Life doesn't always unfold like a Disney fairytale, but we have

133

the power to shape our today and tomorrow. While we cannot change the past, we can learn from our mistakes and actively work on becoming the best versions of ourselves.

It is important to acknowledge our mistakes, as they provide valuable opportunities for reflection, healing, and personal growth. Although I could have expanded the list of regrets in this section, doing so would have diminished the significance of the ones I have shared. Regret is a universal experience, and we all have aspects of our lives that we wish we could change.

No matter what challenges you face in life, remember that things will improve. Maintain a positive mindset, learn from your mistakes, and prioritize personal growth. Strive to be the best version of yourself, as we are all human and prone to making errors.

Chapter 15: Final thoughts

"A measure of intelligence is the ability to change" - Albert Einstein

First and foremost, I express my gratitude for your decision to read this book. As a first-time author, I am genuinely pleased with the outcome and hope that you can extract valuable insights from its contents to bring about significant changes and improve your overall life. Reflecting on my younger self, I often wonder how different my life would have been if I had possessed the knowledge and wisdom contained within these pages back then. This book not only imparts fundamental sales principles but also delivers life lessons on how to utilize sales techniques to enhance various aspects of your life, including personal relationships, career, and finances.

Mastering the art of selling can truly propel you further in your day-to-day interactions. Let me share an example from my recent experience. Just yesterday, one of our vehicles broke down, and when I called the dealership, I was informed that they were overwhelmed with a backlog of over 30 days for repairs and had no loaner cars available. While many people would have accepted this outcome and tried to make the best of it, my knowledge of sales and business prompted me to request a conversation with the general manager of the dealership.

Initially, I was redirected to the service manager, who reiterated the same unacceptable waiting period. I explained to him that this response was simply not satisfactory, emphasizing that such treatment would be detrimental to any business. Determined to address the issue, I insisted on speaking with the general manager. Although he was initially unavailable, I left my contact information and expressed my expectation for a return call by noon. Surprisingly, at 9:30 am, Brian, the general manager, contacted me. I conveyed my concerns to him, emphasizing that it was unreasonable for someone with a vehicle under warranty to be relegated to the back of the queue for servicing. Drawing from my own experience in customer relations, I highlighted the importance of treating people with respect and providing adequate solutions. Recognizing the mishandling of the situation, Brian assured me that the vehicle would be promptly examined, and although loaners were unavailable, he would arrange a rental car at their expense until the issue with our vehicle was resolved.

Had I given up and accepted the initial response, my vehicle would have sat there for a month, accompanied by lease payments for a non-functional vehicle and the costly burden of renting a car for 30 days, especially in the current post-COVID rental market. The teachings embedded in this story revolve around mindset and effective communication. Understanding what can be achieved through proper communication adds tremendous value to one's life. Many individuals and businesses establish boundaries, and most people tend to accept and live within those boundaries. However, what I have shared in this book can be likened to a powerful tool or cheat code that enables you to effectively convey your point of view and achieve better outcomes in various interactions.

When encountering individuals or businesses that fail to respect and work with you on your requests, it may be an indication that they are not the type of people or businesses you want to engage with moving forward. I strongly believe in the principle of treating others as I would like to be treated. Consequently, when a customer expresses concerns about one of my agents, I personally take the call, listen attentively, express empathy, and provide them with a range of options to improve their situation. Likewise, I anticipate receiving the same level of consideration when I advocate for matters that do not sit well with me. Remarkably, there are numerous aspects of life that are open to negotiation. The only way to find out is by making an effort, utilizing the skills at your disposal, and confidently asking for what you believe you deserve from a given situation.

The potential outcomes of these approaches may surprise you. By employing these strategies and seeking what you deserve, you can navigate various aspects of your life more effectively and positively.

In my perspective, it holds great significance to thoroughly examine chapters fourteen, nine, four, and one. These chapters, in my opinion, contain the most crucial information within the book. Chapter fourteen delves into my regrets, drawing from the valuable lessons I've learned by observing the mistakes of those around me. Particularly, my older brother's teenage troubles served as a poignant example. Witnessing the consequences of his actions instilled in me a strong desire to avoid similar regrets for myself and my mother. By reading about my mistakes, my sincere hope is that you will learn from them and establish personal guidelines to steer clear of following in my footsteps.

Chapter nine explores the power of positive thinking, which, in my view, is one of the most transformative practices in my life. Maintaining a positive mindset, even in the face of adversity, has been instrumental in shaping my journey. The more positivity you embrace, the greater your chances of achieving success.

Chapter four focuses on the art of relationship building, a pivotal aspect of the sales process. Even if you're not directly involved in sales, acquiring the skills to foster and nurture relationships can significantly impact your life.

Chapter one serves as the foundation for everything discussed in the book. It emphasizes the notion that you miss out on 100% of the opportunities you don't seize. Taking action is paramount. Personally, I would rather take action and experience failure than live with the regret of never having taken a chance. If fear of failure hinders your progress, it is crucial to address that fear head-on. Once you possess the knowledge and ability, all that remains is summoning the courage to embark on your journey.

If I hadn't taken action in my own life, I would still be working in management at T-Mobile USA, earning a comfortable living but devoid of the fulfilling life I currently enjoy. I consider myself fortunate to have had the support of numerous individuals who played a significant role in shaping who I am today. However, without taking action, their guidance would not have led to my current success. While failure was a possibility, I knew that I could always return to a sales job elsewhere, earning a comparable income. Yet, had I not pursued my aspirations, I would have forever wondered about the potential trajectory of my life.

I draw inspiration from stories like that of Ray Kroc, who encountered numerous failed business ideas before finding the McDonald brothers. He never allowed setbacks to deter him, persistently pursuing opportunities until he found the right one. Notably, Ray possessed a remarkable talent for surrounding himself with capable individuals. Surprisingly, it was not his own idea to acquire the land beneath the McDonald's restaurants, a strategic move that catapulted McDonald's from success to extraordinary profitability. Today, McDonald's stands as the sixth-largest real estate owner globally.

When engaging with a valuable book or educational material, it is unlikely that one will implement every single aspect discussed. However, it is crucial to extract at least one key element and take action upon it. Merely reading without incorporating any changes into one's life, career, or business renders the entire endeavor futile and a waste of time. Therefore, I encourage you to participate in an exercise that I personally undertake whenever I attend a class, watch a training video, or read an educational book.

1. Allocate a dedicated fifteen-minute period for introspection and contemplation regarding the book's content

2. Document your top ten key insights or takeaways that you deem most significant from the book.

3. Condense the list to three to five actionable takeaways that resonate with you the most.

4. Delve deeper into these chosen takeaways and develop a concrete action plan outlining how you will integrate them into your daily life, finances, or career.

5. Implement the action plan by actively taking steps to put your insights into practice. Remember, as emphasized in chapter one, taking action is crucial. Without it, both this exercise and the time invested in reading the book would become entirely unproductive.

As individuals, it is our shared aspiration to continually enhance ourselves. My sincere desire is that this book provides immense value, enabling you to augment your income. Once you have achieved financial growth, the next step is to focus on attaining financial freedom.

My personal plan entails paying off most of my units, accumulating substantial funds in my stocks and crypto accounts, and either passing on or selling my business by the time I reach the age of fifty. This retirement age might hold different significance for me compared to others. For me, retirement from real estate means exploring new business ventures, investing in other enterprises, honing my golf skills, or engaging in activities that capture my interest.

Sales and investing granted me the flexibility to spend more quality time with my children, friends, and family. Although I am not perfect at balancing work and personal life, I am improving. Additionally, these pursuits afford me a comfortable living situation, reliable vehicles, and memorable vacations. Despite this, I still consider myself cash poor in comparison to those who have achieved significant gains in stocks or crypto. Real estate investing may lack immediate liquidity, but its true value lies in equity and residual income.

I intend to write subsequent books centered around investing, real estate, and my personal favorite, self-improvement. To all those who have diligently read this book cover to cover, I extend my heartfelt gratitude. I hope the content was engaging and that you have gained valuable and actionable insights to implement into your own life.